NORFOLK'S OWN
COOKBOOK
EVERYTHING
STOPS
FOR TEA

MARY KEMP   MELINDA RAKER   VANESSA SCOTT

NORFOLK'S OWN
COOKBOOK
EVERYTHING
STOPS
FOR TEA

Recipe photography by Keiron Tovell
Supporting images supplied by the contributors

COOK'S NOTES

We recommend the use of:
Free-range eggs
Unwaxed citrus fruit – if waxed and to be used
whole or for zesting then scrub thoroughly

The following apply unless otherwise stated:
Butter is salted
Freshly ground pepper is black
Spoon measures are level

A CIP catalogue record for this book is available
from the British Library

ISBN 978-0-9931779

contents

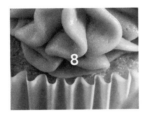

preface

Marie Curie provides high quality nursing care, completely free of charge, to give people with terminal cancer and other illnesses the choice of dying at home, supported by their families, in Norfolk and throughout the UK through our nationwide network of over two thousand Marie Curie nurses. There are also nine Marie Curie Hospices across the UK, providing vital support to patients and families at this most difficult time.

All the sale proceeds of this book will go to help us care for and support more people with terminal illnesses and their families in Norfolk, in partnership with others, including the new North Norfolk Hospice, Tapping House, and the NHS.

I do hope you enjoy these recipes. They will, perhaps, be made all the more delicious by the fact that your purchase is helping us to provide invaluable support to terminally ill people and their loved ones.

Jane Collins
Chief Executive
MARIE CURIE

This excellent book is the result of much hard work and the amazing generosity of two remarkable women from the food industry in Norfolk: Vanessa Scott and Mary Kemp. They have dedicated countless hours and a huge amount of work, at no cost, for over eighteen months, contacting contributors and ensuring that top professionals are involved with the design, editing and photography. They have trialled the recipes, cooked for the photo shoots, publicised Norfolk's Own Cookbook and prepared for its launch. Incredibly busy people in their own right, they undertook this project to raise funds for a very special charity. We can never truly thank them sufficiently for their generosity of spirit and the gift of their time and expertise. Ness and Mary, you are special people indeed and this book is a tribute to you both. We hope that just briefly you might have a few days when 'Everything stops for tea' and you can reflect on this marvellous achievement.

Dr Iain Brooksby
Melinda Raker
Patrons
MARIE CURIE NORFOLK

Alexandra Evans,
Marie Curie nurse

I'm very proud of being a Marie Curie Registered Nurse. I love it when people ask me, 'What do you do?' When I tell them, the first thing they say is, how lovely – but it must be depressing. I then have to explain that although my job can be sad, it is anything but depressing.

Marie Curie nurses make a real difference. We give platinum-standard end-of-life care for people with all terminal illnesses, and the service is free to patients.

I work overnight in the community dedicating myself to my patient on a one-to-one basis and supporting their family. I identify, predict and address my patient's needs, thus allowing them to fulfil their wish to die peacefully and with dignity in their own home.

My job can be funny, sad, frustrating, rewarding, exhausting, exhilarating and sometimes a bit frightening but it is never, ever, depressing and I consider myself privileged to do it.

Thank you for buying this book, and thank you for supporting Marie Curie.

Alexandra Evans
MARIE CURIE NURSE

sweet

Raspberry meringues with raspberry curd

Galton started his career selling home produce on a market stall – the phenomenally successful Galton's Goodies. He went on to work with John Tovey at Millar Howe in the Lake District, which was essentially his training and where he worked his way up to head chef. It was here that Galton met his wife Tracy. Born and bred in Norfolk, Galton always wanted to return, and after some searching found and bought Morston Hall in 1992. He achieved a Michelin star in 1999 and has 3 AA rosettes.

Galton and Tracy Blackiston, Morston Hall, Holt

makes 6

MERINGUES
80g egg whites
80g caster sugar, sifted
80g icing sugar, sifted
Freeze-dried raspberries
Whipped cream and fresh
  raspberries, to serve

RASPBERRY CURD
250g raspberry purée
  (see bottom of page)
1 medium egg
3 medium egg yolks
150g caster sugar
75g unsalted butter

Preheat the oven to 100°C/fan 80°C/gas ¼. Line a baking tray with baking parchment.

Place the egg whites into the spotlessly clean bowl of a food mixer and whisk at high speed until they form soft peaks. While continuing to whisk, very slowly add the caster sugar. Remove the bowl from the mixer and, using a metal slotted spoon, carefully fold in the icing sugar.

Pipe or spoon the meringue mixture on to the lined baking tray, sprinkle over some freeze dried raspberries and cook in the centre of the oven for 1 hour. Remove from the oven and place on to a rack to cool.

For the curd, whisk together the raspberry purée, egg, egg yolks and sugar. Place the bowl over a saucepan of gently simmering water, making sure that the bottom of the bowl does not touch the water, and continue to whisk until the mixture thickens. Remove from the heat, whisk the butter into the warm mixture and pass through a sieve into a bowl. Place a piece of cling film down on to the mixture to prevent a skin forming, and allow to cool.

Serve the meringues with a filling of raspberry curd, whipped cream and fresh raspberries.

For the raspberry purée, whizz fresh raspberries in a food processor or liquidiser, then pass through a fine sieve. This freezes well and can be sweetened to taste with sugar syrup to accompany other desserts.

Norfolk saffron mini madeleines

'North Norfolk was once famous for its wonderful saffron and there was a lucrative export trade to the Low Countries. Tudor, Stuart and Georgian growers ranged from large estates to individuals, including a vicar of Blakeney, who produced the crop as a sideline. Today, after an absence of over two centuries, saffron is thriving again. A birthday present of twenty plants from my mother sparked my interest in the spice. A few years later we planted twenty thousand, all by hand, at our family smallholding at Burnham Norton, and began commercial production. Our award-winning saffron is prized for its for strength and quality. This recipe includes our unique saffron flour, a ready-to-use blend of flour and hand-ground Norfolk saffron.'

Dr Sally Francis, Norfolk Saffron

makes 48

100g butter, soft
100g caster sugar
2 large eggs
100g Norfolk Saffron
self-raising flour
Icing sugar, for dusting

Preheat the oven to 190°C/fan 170°C/gas 5. Spray two 24-hole mini madeleine moulds with cake-release spray or lightly oil them.

In a mixing bowl, cream the butter and sugar together, then beat in the eggs.

Sift the flour into the bowl and fold into the butter mixture. Tip any little pieces of saffron trapped in the sieve back into the mixing bowl.

Fill the moulds with the mixture using a piping bag. Scrape off the excess using the edge of a palette knife so that the mixture fills each indentation and is flush with the top of the mould.

Bake for 12–15 minutes until golden brown. Leave to cool in the tins for a couple of minutes, then carefully prise the madeleines out. Leave to cool on a wire rack. Dust with icing sugar.

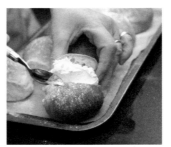

Norfolk splits with cream & strawberry jam

'Inspired by the wonderful, mouth-watering Cornish and Devon splits with a light and airy texture, our soft crusts are sinfully filled to the brim with dollops of luscious Norfolk double cream and homemade strawberry jam. We make the dough by hand using best quality ingredients: flour, yeast, whole milk and butter, all sourced locally from some of the finest Norfolk producers and baked so they are fresh and ready to be served warm for tea. For me this is what old-fashioned teatime is all about.'

Susan Hudson, Bread Workshops

makes 12

SPLITS

10g fresh yeast

210g whole milk, warm, plus extra
    if needed

½ tsp sugar

55g unsalted butter, diced

350g white bread flour, plus extra
    for dusting

7g salt

Icing sugar, for dusting

FILLING

300ml double cream, whipped

Homemade strawberry jam
    or a good quality local one

Line a baking tray with baking parchment.

Crumble the fresh yeast into a bowl, cream it to a paste with a little milk, then add the sugar.

Rub the butter into the flour, mixing in the salt, until the mixture resembles fine crumbs. Add the yeast liquid and rest of the milk and combine to make a soft dough. If the dough is too wet, add a little more flour; if too dry, add a little more milk.

Turn the dough out on a lightly floured surface and knead for 10 minutes.

Clean the mixing bowl, return the dough to it, cover and leave at room temperature until doubled in size – this can take 1–1½ hours.

Turn the dough out on to a freshly floured work surface, gently knead to dispel the air, then make into a long sausage. Divide this into 12 equal portions and shape them into rolls by rolling the dough under your cupped hand. Arrange the rolls closely together on the baking tray.

Allow the rolls to prove, covered with a tea towel, for about 40 minutes or until they have almost doubled in size.

Preheat the oven to 220°C/200°C/gas 7.

Bake for 15–20 minutes until golden. Once out of the oven, dust with icing sugar and cover with a clean tea towel to keep the crusts soft.

To serve cut across the buns at an angle and fill with generous dollops of double cream and strawberry jam.

'Thunder and lightning' is a split filled with double cream and golden syrup. Eat splits on the day or freeze for one month.

Norfolk Ale fruit loaf

Brewing was traditionally a woman's job carried out by 'alewives' or 'brewsters', and it was these ladies who inspired Jo to start her own brewery. Jo – 'the bird who brews' – is Norfolk's only female brewster. She began brewing in 2010 and her brewery is housed in a disused farm building on the Barsham Estate near Fakenham. She has gone from strength to strength, brewing three distinctive craft beers which are available in cask, bottle and five-litre mini-casks. Her beer is served over the bar at pubs across East Anglia and London. Mum-of-two Jo is married to Kiwi hotelier Chris Coubrough.

Jo Coubrough, Jo C's Norfolk Ale

makes a 500g loaf

Butter, for greasing

300ml Jo C's Norfolk Ale Bitter Old Bustard

2 oranges, zest

140g raisins

140g sultanas

140g brown sugar

280g self-raising flour

½ tsp mixed spice

Preheat the oven to 150°C/130°fan/gas 2. Butter a small (450g/500g) loaf tin and line with baking parchment.

Warm the ale, zest, raisins, sultanas and sugar in a saucepan, then take the pan from the heat and leave the fruit to infuse for a good 10 minutes.

Stir in the flour and spice into a bowl, add the fruit mix and stir well to combine. Pour the mixture into the prepared tin. Bake for 60–80 minutes, until a skewer inserted into the middle of the loaf comes out clean. Leave in the tin for 10 minutes before turning out into a wire rack.

Slice and serve warm, with butter.

This simple recipe is also delicious topped with a sharp wild berry jam or a slice of cheese.

Morning muffins

'Based in Swaffham, we feed staff in the workplace and children at school, which brings us all sorts of interesting food challenges. Our ethos is to use fresh ingredients to produce home-cooked meals with heart to keep all our customers happy. Our morning muffin was created to have something wholesome but delicious and easy to make for our busy chefs, who have a huge workload in the mornings. We wanted something that could compete with the traditional hot breakfast products and routine bakery range, a muffin for those with sophisticated tastes. Needless to say, these muffins are good at any time of day.'

Edwards & Blake

makes 12

MUFFINS

2 medium eggs

225g soft light brown sugar

160ml rapeseed oil

300g bananas, mashed

150g fresh or tinned pineapple, finely chopped

125g sultanas

40g oats

260g plain flour

10g poppy seeds

2 tsp bicarbonate of soda

1 tsp ground cinnamon

1 tsp ground ginger

TOPPING

4 tbsp mixed sunflower seeds, pumpkin seeds, linseeds and oats

Demerara sugar, to taste

Preheat the oven to 160°C/fan 140°C/gas 3. Line a 12-hole muffin tray with tulip cases.

With an electric whisk, beat the eggs and sugar until pale and fluffy. Still whisking, pour in the oil in a slow, steady stream. Then, by hand, gently fold in the banana, pineapple and sultanas, moving the spoon in figure-of-8 movements.

Fold in the rest of the dry ingredients with care (more care = more air = better rise), then spoon the mixture into the tulip cases until two-thirds full, allowing room for a good rise.

Mix the topping ingredients together, sprinkle over the muffins and bake for 20–25 minutes until risen and firm. Serve warm.

Serve with a strong coffee or a mug of tea. Or warm for a few seconds in a microwave and serve with butterscotch sauce and thick cream or crème fraîche for a cheat's sticky toffee pudding.

Sticky citrus & polenta muffins

In the Yare Valley, nestled beside the Norfolk broads, the Mack family have been working the rich fertile land of their farm for over 100 years. Rapeseed has been grown across their fields for many years and has become an important part of their farming, along with potatoes, sugar beet and cereals. This incredibly versatile British oil is harvested, pressed and bottled on site by mechanical means and twice filtered to retain its natural health properties. Its deliciously subtle flavour makes it an ideal option for everyday cooking, including both sweet and savoury dishes.

Yare Valley Oils

makes 9

MUFFINS

250ml Yare Valley rapeseed oil

250g golden granulated sugar

3 medium eggs

250g ground almonds

125g fine polenta

5g salt

5g gluten-free baking powder
   or ½ tsp bicarbonate of soda
   and ½ tsp cream of tartar

3 limes, zest
   (use juice for glaze, below)

1 lemon, zest
   (use juice for glaze, below)

SYRUP GLAZE

3 limes, juice

1 lemon, juice

3 tbsp Norfolk honey

ICING

150g cream cheese

50g icing sugar, sifted

1 lime, zest and juice

Preheat the oven to 150°C/fan 130°C/gas 2. Put 9 tulip muffin cases into a muffin tray.

In a food processor, mix the oil and sugar until creamy. Beat in the eggs one by one.

In a clean bowl, mix together the dry ingredients with the lime and lemon zest and fold into the oil mixture. Put the lemon and limes to one side to make the syrup glaze.

Fill the muffin cases almost to the top (note that there is very little rise in these cakes) and bake for 1 hour, until a skewer inserted into the centre comes out clean.

While the muffins are cooking, make the syrup glaze. Mix the juice of the lemon and limes with the honey in a small heavy pan and boil together until reduced by half and syrupy. When the muffins come out of the oven, pour the warmed citrus syrup over them and allow it to soak into the little cakes.
Leave to cool on a wire rack.

Meanwhile, beat the cream cheese and icing sugar together and add most of the lime zest (reserve some for the tops) and 3 tablespoons of lime juice. Ice the muffins when completely cool. Decorate the top with lime zest.

These moist little cakes will keep for 5 days in a fridge. Bring up to room temperature to enjoy at their best.

Fig & apricot scones

'Our tea-shop dream finally came true in August 2011, in the idyllic Norfolk village of Heydon, where it really is like stepping back in time. A charming and totally unspoilt cluster of picture-postcard cottages, our tea shop, the artisan bakery, pub, hairdresser's and church surround the picturesque village green with its well. I have wonderful childhood memories of baking with my mum and nanas, which is where my love of baking comes from. Almost everything we serve is made by us on the premises with seasonal ingredients sourced from local producers. Our aim is for you to love the experience you have with us.'

Cindy Watson, Heydon Tea Rooms

makes 10 generous-sized

SCONES
600g self-raising flour
60g caster sugar
90g dried figs, chopped
90g dried apricots, chopped
60g soft butter
2 tsp ground cinnamon
2 tsp baking powder
150ml milk
2 medium eggs

GLAZE
1 egg, beaten
2 tbsp Demerara sugar

Preheat the oven to 200°C/180°/gas 6. Line a baking tray with baking parchment.

Place all ingredients in a large bowl and bring together with a knife.

Tip the dough on to a lightly floured surface and roll out to a thickness of approximately 4cm. Cut into rounds using a large cutter or mug, and place on the prepared baking sheet.

Brush the scones with the egg wash and sprinkle with Demerara sugar. Bake for around 12 minutes, until golden brown and well risen.

Enjoy with jam and clotted cream.

Funfetti cupcakes

'Buns of Fun began life in 2010, baking cakes for beach picnics in beautiful North Norfolk, when my eldest son was tiny. From themed cupcakes with cute toppers to gigantic creations such as the Gingerbread House at Holkham Hall, our produce has been driven by customer demand. Buns of Fun have produced in excess of 8,500 cakes and cupcakes to date and I've loved every one, as well as producing another baby Bun. My Funfetti Cupcake recipe is a white cake with white buttercream, which my boys love. Confetti sugar sprinkles inside add surprise, and the coloured sugar vermicelli and glitter add glamour.'

Emma Thorburn, Buns of Fun

makes 12 regular or 24 minis

CUPCAKES
215g plain flour
½ tsp baking powder
¼ tsp baking soda
½ tsp salt
250g unsalted butter
200g granulated sugar
1 large egg
60ml yoghurt (plain or vanilla,
    or Greek) or sour cream
170ml whole milk or soy
    or almond milk
2 tsp vanilla extract
100g rainbow sprinkles

BUTTERCREAM
170g unsalted butter, soft
360g icing sugar, sifted
60ml cream
2 tsp vanilla extract
Sugar vermicelli and edible glitter

Preheat the oven to 180°C/fan 160°C/gas 4. Place 12 cupcake cases in a muffin tray or use petit four cases to make 24 small muffins.

Sift together all the dry ingredients until well combined.

Melt the butter, then whisk in the sugar. It will look sandy. Cool in the fridge for a few minutes.

Use a fork to combine the wet ingredients: the egg, yoghurt, milk and vanilla extract, together with the cooled butter and sugar mix. Fold into the dry ingredients and stir until the mixture is the consistency of a smooth thick batter.

Fold in the sprinkles gently but quickly. Don't overdo them or the colours will run. Fill the cases two-thirds full and bake for 15–20 minutes. If making mini cupcakes, bake for 8–9 minutes until a skewer inserted in the middle comes out clean. Place on a wire rack to cool.

For the buttercream, using a food mixer on medium speed, beat the softened butter for around 3 minutes until smooth and creamy. Add the icing sugar, cream and vanilla extract and beat on a slow setting for 1 minute, then increase to the maximum speed for 3–4 minutes. Add more icing sugar if the buttercream is too thin, or more cream if too thick. Place in a piping bag with a star nozzle and have fun piping – then go bonkers with sprinkles and glitter.

Use mixed colours of edible glitter if you really want to shine.

Raspberry trifle cupcakes

'We are a firm of chartered accountants, established in the region for almost 100 years. Food has brought people together throughout history and this is the case at our business. Special occasions are when the keen bakers and cooks at the firm bring in their delicious homemade treats, and with each passing year the bar is raised higher. I always try to use local produce in my baking, happy in the knowledge that the raspberries and jam used in my recipe will likely have been sourced from clients, friends and family.'

Sharon Corke, M&A Partners, Norwich

makes 12

CUPCAKES
80g unsalted butter, soft
280g caster sugar
240g plain flour
1 tbsp baking powder
¼ tsp salt
240ml whole milk
1 tsp vanilla extract
2 medium eggs

FILLING AND TOPPING
450ml double cream
½ tsp vanilla extract
6 medium egg yolks
2 tbsp caster sugar
50g cornflour
24–32 fresh raspberries
Raspberry jam

Place a teaspoon of Madeira in the scooped-out case before filling to give a boozy cake.

Preheat the oven to 190°C/fan 170°C/gas 5. Line a 12-hole muffin tray with tulip cases.

Using an electric whisk on a low speed, beat the butter, sugar, flour, baking powder and salt until they resemble fine breadcrumbs.

In a jug and using a fork, whisk together the milk, vanilla extract and eggs. Pour three-quarters of the mixture into the dry ingredients while mixing on a low speed. When combined, add the rest of the liquid and mix until smooth.

Fill each muffin case two-thirds full. Bake for 18–20 minutes or until the sponges bounce back when pressed. Leave to cool on a wire rack.

For the custard filling, put the cream in a saucepan with the vanilla extract and bring to the boil; in a separate bowl mix together the egg yolks, sugar and cornflour into a paste.

When the cream has come to the boil, take it off the heat and pour a little into the egg and cornflour paste. Stir well, then pour into the cream left in the pan and return to the heat. Heat through, stirring constantly with a wooden spoon to prevent the bottom from catching and the eggs from scrambling. Continue to cook gently for a further minute to ensure the cornflour is fully cooked. Pour into a jug, cover with cling film and allow to cool for 30–40 minutes.

Using a cupcake plunger or a sharp knife, make a hollow in the centre of each cake. Keep the cut-out pieces to one side. Place a raspberry or two in the hollow, spoon in ½ teaspoon of jam, then ½ teaspoon of custard, then replace the cut-out pieces, trimming to fit and pressing down gently until level. Spoon or pipe the custard on top, and finish with a fresh raspberry.

Lavender cupcakes

'The Blakeney Hotel has one of the most enviable views of the North Norfolk coastline. It is an ideal spot to relax and enjoy tasty homemade food. With all our recipes we try to encompass everything that is wonderful about our glorious coastline and natural habitat. We use fresh, locally sourced ingredients whenever possible. These cupcakes are very popular because not only are they delicious but they are extremely light and fluffy with a subtle hint of Norfolk lavender.'

The Blakeney Hotel

makes 18 small or 9 large

LAVENDER-INFUSED MILK

205ml whole milk

5 tbsp lavender buds

CUPCAKES

60g butter

180g plain flour

210g caster sugar

2¼ tsp baking powder

180ml lavender-infused milk
(see above)

2 medium eggs

BUTTERCREAM

125g unsalted butter, soft

250g icing sugar

1 tsp vanilla extract

A few drops of purple food
colouring

25ml lavender-infused milk
(see above)

Infuse the milk with the lavender by leaving the buds in the milk overnight in the fridge. The following day, strain the milk ready to use in the sponge and the buttercream.

Preheat the oven to 170°C/fan 150°C/gas 3. Line a cupcake baking tray with 18 small paper cases or 9 large.

Put the butter, plain flour, caster sugar and baking powder in a large bowl and, using a handheld electric whisk, beat on a slow speed until everything is well combined. Slowly pour in 180ml lavender-infused milk, continuing to beat until well mixed in. Add the eggs and beat again.

Fill the paper cases with the mixture to two-thirds full. Bake for 15–20 minutes until the sponge is springy to the touch and a skewer inserted in the centre comes out clean.

Turn the cupcakes out of the baking tray straight away to avoid them drying and leave to cool on a wire rack.

For the buttercream, beat the butter, icing sugar, vanilla extract and food colour with a hand-held electric whisk. Add the 25ml lavender-infused milk and beat again until fully combined, light and creamy. Pipe in rosettes on top of each cupcake.

Make sure the lavender you use is of an edible grade from a reputable supplier or from a garden where you can be certain it hasn't been sprayed with harmful chemicals.

Blondies

The Norfolk Mead hotel in Coltishall is situated alongside the famous national park of the Norfolk Broads with its wonderful mixture of open water, woodland, fen and marsh, unique birdlife and wildfowl, and over 300 kilometres of footpaths. Anna and James met and married when they were working for McLaren on the Formula 1 circuit ten years ago, travelling the world and catering for the drivers, mechanics and support team. They had always dreamed of owning their own hotel and venue, and the Norfolk Mead is the realisation of that dream. 'This recipe makes a delightfully rich, sweet teatime treat. Quick and easy, it's best made by hand.'

Anna Duttson and James Holliday, owners of The Norfolk Mead

serves 10

200g unsalted butter

450g light muscovado sugar

2 medium eggs

1 medium egg yolk

3 tsp vanilla extract

280g plain flour

Pinch salt

170g toasted pecan nuts, coarsely chopped

Preheat the oven to 180°C/fan 160°C/gas 4. Butter an 18x32cm tin, then line with baking parchment.

In a saucepan over a low heat, gently melt the butter and blend in the sugar until dissolved, cooking and stirring for 1 minute and being careful not to let the mixture boil. Leave to cool for 10 minutes.

Whisk the whole eggs and egg yolk together, then add the vanilla extract and pour into the cooked sugar mix. Fold in the flour, salt and nuts and stir until thoroughly combined, then spoon into the prepared tin.

Bake for 20–25 minutes until light golden brown.

Try adding chocolate chips, and/or dried fruit soaked in liqueur, whisky or rum.

Bitter chocolate & kirsch cherry tortes

'These delicious little moist tortes are made from a smooth batter which is then baked in moulds. This is the teatime treat when you are pushed for time or simply feeling lazy, yet the combination of bitter chocolate, cherry and kirsch flavours make them a real indulgence. The recipe calls for cherry jam and kirsch cherries. Obviously, if you have the time, making your own jam is ideal, but there is nothing wrong with using a good quality bought jam. Soaking your own cherries in kirsch is extremely easy, however.'

Lewis Peck, head chef at The Last Brasserie, Norwich

makes 12

250g unsalted butter

5 tbsp cherry jam

2 lemons, zest

75g cocoa powder

300g caster sugar

3 medium eggs, beaten

100g plain flour, sifted

Kirsch-soaked cherries, to garnish

In the summer months, these tortes would also be delicious made with raspberry jam and topped with fresh raspberries.

Preheat the oven to 160°C/140°C/gas 3. Fill a 12-hole muffin tray with tulip cases.

Melt the butter and jam over a medium heat, then add the lemon zest, cocoa powder and sugar, stirring constantly.

As soon as this has all combined, slowly add the beaten eggs. It is important not to put them all in at once otherwise the mixture will cool too much and split.

Remove the pan from the heat and carefully fold in the flour, a little at a time, making sure the batter remains smooth. Pour the mixture into the cases and bake for 20–25 minutes.

Garnish each torte with kirsch cherries. Serve warm with ice cream or clotted cream.

Pistachio & white chocolate shortbread

'After studying professional cookery at college for three years I am now focusing on cakes and pastries. I work locally as a pastry chef where I am able to use all the skills I have learned making cakes and pastries for visitors to Norwich. These cookies are easy to make, a quick and tasty teatime treat. They offer a contrast of textures with sweet white chocolate and crunchy toasted nuts. If you want to vary them, substitute the white chocolate with dried fruit such as cranberries or sour cherries, or replace the pistachios with toasted hazelnuts to make your own favourite cookie.'

Bethany Redhead, young chef

This recipe has been sponsored by a Norfolk Charitable Trust

makes 18

100g shelled pistachio nuts
200g butter, soft
100g caster sugar
260g plain flour
40g cornflour
100g white chocolate,
  roughly chopped

Preheat the oven to 160oC/fan 140°C/gas 3. Line a baking tray with baking parchment.

Roughly chop the pistachios and toast in a hot pan to lightly brown them.

Rub the softened butter, sugar, flour and cornflour together. When the ingredients become like breadcrumbs, add the toasted pistachios and the white chocolate. Continue to work the mixture together until it forms a dough.

Take tablespoon-sized pieces of the dough, mould into balls and press between your hands to form round shortbreads. Arrange on the baking tray with space between and bake for 15–20 minutes until slightly golden in colour.

Remove from the oven and allow to cool completely on the tray. Store in an airtight biscuit jar or container.

Dipping the final cooled biscuit in a little melted white chocolate and sprinkling with more of the chopped nuts is the OTT version.

Lemon macarons

Where better to enjoy afternoon tea than in the beautiful surroundings of Congham Hall? It sits in 30 acres of parkland, including orchards and a renowned herb garden stocked with over 400 varieties. The gardens provide produce for the restaurant tables, harvested daily by the chefs, and cut flowers to scent the rooms. With the emphasis on creative and delicious food at Congham, the head chef hopes you will enjoy his delicious teatime recipe.

Nick Claxton-Webb, head chef at Congham Hall

makes 16

MACARONS

4 large egg whites

80g caster sugar

220g icing sugar

120g ground almonds

2 lemons, zest, and juice of 1

3 or 4 drops yellow food colouring

LEMON CURD

100g caster sugar

2 large eggs

2 large egg yolks

2 lemons, zest and juice

100g unsalted butter, soft

Gel food colours give a more intense colour and are available in good cook shops and most supermarkets now.

Preheat the oven to 180°C/fan 160°C/gas 4. Line 2 large baking sheets with baking parchment.

With an electric whisk, beat the egg whites to stiff peaks. Add the caster sugar 1 spoonful at a time and keep whisking until the sugar has dissolved and the mixture is thick, smooth and glossy, with no graininess when you test it between your fingers.

Sift together the icing sugar and the ground almonds into a separate bowl. Next add the lemon zest, juice and the food colouring. Gently fold in a third of the meringue to loosen the mixture, then slowly and gently fold in the remainder, being careful not to overmix.

Carefully spoon the mixture into a piping bag fitted with a medium plain nozzle. Pipe discs on to the prepared trays $1^1/_2$ -2cm in diameter; be sure to leave plenty of room between the macarons as they will spread. Leave the tray out at room temperature for 20 minutes to allow a skin to form. This is weather dependent and will take longer if the atmosphere is very moist. This standing process allows the macarons to rise evenly, as well as ensuring the frilly 'feet' form at the base. Bake for 10–15 minutes. Allow to cool on the tray then carefully remove.

For the lemon curd, place the caster sugar, whole eggs, egg yolks and lemon zest and juice into a heatproof bowl and place the bowl over a pan of hot water on a low heat – make sure the bottom of the bowl does not touch the water in the pan. Whisk the mixture until it thickens. Next slowly whisk in the butter until the curd is smooth and has reached coating consistency. Set aside to cool, then chill.

To assemble, spoon the curd into a piping bag. Pipe the curd on to the bottom of one macaron and place the bottom of another on top to form a sandwich. Unfilled macarons will keep in an airtight container for about a week; however, filled ones are best eaten within a few hours of assembling.

Lemon-frosted pistachio cake

'This recipe was always for an occasion and therefore special. Often requested by husband, children and grandchildren, it was treated with a certain amount of excitement and was demolished almost immediately. During Jenny's last days, after a long and heroic fight against cancer, the role of the Marie Curie nurses was remarkable. Their steady professional presence, timely and gentle care meant that Jenny's last hours were comfortable and dignified, which in turn allowed us to make the most of our final time with a remarkable lady. So how fitting to share Jenny's special cake with Marie Curie – it will be enjoyed.'

Stuart Woodhead, in memory of his wife

serves 6–8

CAKE
250g butter, soft
250g caster sugar
3 medium eggs
100g shelled pistachio nuts
100g ground almonds
1 orange, zest and juice
1 tsp rosewater
60g plain flour
ICING
100g icing sugar
2 tbsp lemon juice
Strands of lemon zest

Preheat the oven to 160°C/fan 140°C/gas 3. Grease a 22cm cake tin and line with baking parchment.

Cream the butter and sugar in a food mixer until light and fluffy. Add the eggs one at a time, beating between each addition.

Blitz the pistachios to fine crumbs in a food processor then add them and the ground almonds to the butter and sugar. Add the zest, juice and rosewater to the mix and fold in the sifted flour until fully combined.

Bake for 1 hour, covering the top lightly with foil for the last 10 minutes to prevent it catching.

To make the icing, mix the sifted icing sugar with the lemon juice, stir until smooth and then pour over the cake. Decorate with lemon zest.

Good for afternoon tea, or served with fruit for a delicious pudding.

Breckland blueberry, lavender & honey cake

Mermaid Sandelson won the junior section of the Great Brecks Bake-off in September 2014. The event, in Swaffham, formed part of the annual Norfolk Food and Drink Festival. The judges, including Vanessa Scott, were so impressed with the cake and the luscious use of local ingredients that she was asked to take part in the cookbook. At only thirteen years old she is our youngest contributor. Mermaid has been helping her mother and sister bake for the Perfect Spot Café in the gardens of Narborough Hall since she was seven, and looks forward to opening her own restaurant one day.

Mermaid Sandelson

serves 8

CAKE

20ml milk

6 lavender sprigs

250g soft butter

200g golden caster sugar

250g self-raising flour

50g runny Breckland honey

5 medium eggs

150g blueberries

FILLING

250g icing sugar

80g soft unsalted butter

30ml lavender milk

50g blueberries

200g Essence Blueberry and Lavender Jam

50g Breckland honey

TOPPING

100g blueberries

1 tbsp Essence Blueberry and Lavender Jam

1 garden lavender sprig

Preheat the oven to 180°C/fan 160°C/gas 4. Line two 20cm sponge tins with baking parchment.

Gently warm 70ml milk with 6 sprigs of lavender and set aside for around 30 minutes to infuse.

Cream the soft butter with the caster sugar and honey until pale and fluffy. Gradually add the eggs, one egg at a time with one tsp of the flour and beat well until all the eggs are combined.

Sift the flour into the cake mixture and fold in gently. At this point add the 150g of the blueberries and 20ml of the infused lavender milk. The blueberries must be barely mixed through, only one or two folds, so they do not break.

Divide the mixture between the two tins and bake for 25 minutes until the centre of the cake is risen and just firm to the touch. Turn out the cakes and very carefully peel off the baking parchment and the blueberries will be slightly sticky on the base.

While the cake is cooling make the filling. Mix the honey gently with 50g of the blueberries and set aside. Whisk the soft butter with the sifted icing sugar until very white and smooth. Take the lavender sprigs out of the milk and add the milk to the butter icing. Whisk again.

When the cake is cool spread one half with a thick layer of the jam and spread the honeyed blueberries on top. Spread the lavender butter cream on the other half and sandwich together.

Decorate the top with the blueberries mixed with the tbsp of jam and a sprig of garden lavender.

Serve on an English summer's afternoon in the garden, surrounded by lavender and bees.

Rapeseed oil, lemon & blackberry cake

The Wildebeest, part of Animal Inns, has been established for over twenty years and is firmly part of the Norfolk food scene, producing not only great food but nurturing passionate young chefs. Food is at the heart of the business, with an emphasis on simple, well-cooked dishes and only the best ingredients, sourced if possible from local suppliers.

The Wildebeest, Norwich

serves 16

400ml rapeseed oil, plus extra
    for oiling
300g ground almonds
50g flaked almonds
370g caster sugar
3 tsp baking powder, sifted
75g fresh white breadcrumbs
8 large eggs
3 lemons, zest
180g blackberries

Preheat the oven to 200°C/fan 180°C/gas 6. Oil a 30cm wide, 3cm deep cake tin with a little rapeseed oil and line with baking parchment.

Mix together the ground almonds, half the flaked almonds, 270g of the caster sugar, the baking powder and breadcrumbs in a large mixing bowl.

Beat in the eggs one by one with a wooden spoon until thoroughly mixed. Add the oil and lemon zest and beat well to combine. Spoon the mix into the prepared tin and bake for 30 minutes.

Remove from the oven and scatter the blackberries and the remaining flaked almonds and caster sugar over the top. Bake for a further 15 minutes until the cake is golden. To test if the cake is ready you can also insert a skewer into the middle of the cake: if it comes out clean, it is cooked.

As well as being great with a cup of tea, this cake makes an excellent pudding with a scoop of ice cream or dollop of yoghurt. Make it with blueberries or raspberries too.

Elveden Estate Guinness & chocolate cake

Arthur Edward Guinness, Lord Iveagh is a descendant of Arthur Guinness, inventor of the stout to which he gave his name. The 23,000-acre estate stretching across Norfolk and Suffolk is a sizeable farming enterprise, but also has a thriving café, restaurant, food and shopping courtyard. Much of the food sold in the shop and café comes from the estate. 'My family have been farming here for more than one hundred years. We Guinnesses have been known as brewers one way or another for nine generations and we are fortunate that our traditional beer goes so well with baking cakes and as a cooking ingredient generally.'

Lord Iveagh, Elveden Estate

serves 10

CAKE

250ml Guinness

250g unsalted butter, plus extra
    for greasing

400g caster sugar

140ml crème fraiche

2 medium eggs

75g cocoa powder

1 dessertspoon vanilla extract

275g plain flour

½ tsp bicarbonate of soda

TOPPING

300g cream cheese

150g icing sugar

125g double cream

Preheat the oven to 180°C/fan 160°C/gas 4. Grease a 22cm cake tin and line with baking parchment.

Warm the Guinness and butter in a pan together until the butter melts, then set aside.

Using an electric hand whisk, cream the sugar, crème fraiche and eggs together in a bowl until well combined. Add the cocoa powder and vanilla extract and mix well, then whisk into the Guinness and butter mixture. Finally fold in the flour and bicarbonate of soda.

Pour the mixture into the tin and bake for around 1 hour; the cake will rise and then fall back in on itself, and this is fine. Leave to cool in the tin on a wire rack.

Soften the cream cheese and sift over the icing sugar, then mix gently until smooth (overworking the cheese will make it runny). In a separate bowl, whip the double cream until it starts to thicken, then combine with the cheese mixture to create a thick icing to top the cake. When the cake is cold, spread on top of the cake to resemble the frothy head on a glass of Guinness.

This is a really simple but still impressive cake with Guinness to keep it moist and add extra flavour – a great make-ahead cake.

Apple crumble cake

After nine years of selling their sponge cakes within Byfords, Holt, Iain Wilson and his partners set up SPONGE in 2010 to sell the cakes to a wider audience. Sue Barrons, with her old-school standards and eye for detail, originally developed the sponge cakes at Byfords that helped make the little café in Norfolk famous. 'We have taken the sponges from Byfords, added a few more family members to the range, improved the recipes even further and added some lovely new packaging. We are now selling to other retailers, cafés, farm shops and even through the post via our website.'

SPONGE

serves 12

CRUMBLE TOPPING
55g plain flour
35g soft dark brown sugar
40g butter
20g chopped walnuts

CAKE
300g soft dark brown sugar
300g self-raising flour, sifted
3 tsp baking powder
3 tsp cinnamon
6 medium eggs
90g sultanas
300ml sunflower oil
350g dessert apples

BRITTLE
150g sugar
4 tbsp water

FILLING
200g mascarpone cheese
1 tsp vanilla extract
1 tbsp runny honey

This crumble cake would also be delicious made with pears.

Preheat the oven to 180°C/160°Cfan /gas 4. Grease and line a 21cm cake tin with baking parchment.

For the topping, combine the flour and sugar, then rub in the butter until the mixture resembles coarse breadcrumbs. Press together with your fingers to create uneven lumps. Scatter the walnuts over and gently pull through the mix. Refrigerate for 20 minutes to firm up.

For the cake, in a medium bowl mix the sugar, self-raising flour, baking powder and cinnamon thoroughly with a wooden spoon. Add the eggs one at a time and continue mixing until well combined. Next add the sultanas and sunflower oil and mix well into a dark brown, batter-like mixture. Peel and roughly chop the apples and add to the sponge mixture.

Fill the lined cake tin, smooth the top and bake for 1 hour. Remove from the oven, scatter the crumble mix over the top and bake for a further 30 minutes until a skewer inserted in the centre comes out clean. If necessary, cover the cake with a sheet of baking parchment to prevent it becoming too brown. Leave to cool on a wire rack.

For the brittle, line a baking tray with baking parchment. Put the sugar and water in a heavy-based shallow pan and place on a medium heat, until golden brown. It is important not to stir the mixture. Pour a thin layer on to the baking parchment and leave to set.

When the cake is completely cool, cut in half. Cream the filling ingredients together gently and use to sandwich the cake. Decorate with the brittle shards.

Sticky pear & ginger cake

The Picnic Fayre Delicatessen set in the Old Forge, Cley, was opened in 1984 by John Pryor and has become a culinary Aladdin's den. When you walk in the door you will be spoilt for choice. Victoria Pryor joined the business sixteen years ago, bringing her amazingly understated skills and knowledge, one of which is the ability to make the most fabulous cakes, and without any fuss or gadgetry. The most important utensils in Vic's kitchen are her wooden spoons and bowls. The cakes on sale are often created without formal recipes but always with an instinctive understanding of what works and what doesn't.

Picnic Fayre, Cley next the Sea

serves 12

2 x 400g tins pear halves, drained
(1 tin: pears kept whole,
1 tin: chopped)

SYRUP
125g butter
300g soft dark brown sugar

CAKE
210g caster sugar
210g soft light brown sugar
425g unsalted butter, soft
Good handful crystallised ginger,
chopped
4 tsp ground ginger
6 eggs, beaten
425g self-raising flour

*Eat warm with cream or leave
to get cold.*

Preheat the oven to 160°C/140°/gas 3. Butter a 25cm wide, 5cm deep springform cake tin and line with baking parchment.

To make the syrup, melt the butter and the dark brown sugar in a pan and bring to the boil. It is important to stir the mixture all the time until it becomes a lovely smooth sauce and the sugar has completely dissolved. Pour the sauce into the cake tin and leave to go hard: 30–45 minutes – this stage is very important.

Arrange the pear halves on the caramel, flat-side down.

To make the cake, cream the sugars and butter together until light and fluffy, then add the crystallised and ground gingers.

Stir in the eggs, then fold in the flour, beating well with a wooden spoon until smooth. Add the chopped pears and stir well to combine.

Pour the cake mixture into the tin and cook for 1 hour. To test, insert a skewer into the centre; if it comes out clean, the cake is cooked.

Leave in the tin for about 20 minutes before turning it out on to a serving dish, with the sticky sauce on top.

Rhubarb & orange cake

'Ceres Bookshop and Tea Room welcomes visitors from all over Norfolk and beyond. Our tea room is quiet, peaceful and cosy in the winter and the garden is the ideal spot for cream tea when the sun is shining. Everybody loves homemade cakes, so when I discovered that Donna who helps me in Ceres has a passion for baking, I knew we were on to a winning partnership. Our cakes vary depending on what is in season, often using locally produced fruits from either mine or Donna's garden or generously donated by loyal customers. This recipe was the result of an abundance of rhubarb and has proved to be one of our most popular cakes.'

Claire Dunne, Ceres Bookshop and Tea Room, Swaffham

serves 10

175g butter, soft

225g golden caster sugar

3 large eggs

100g self-raising flour

2 oranges, zest

175g ground almonds

400g rhubarb, trimmed and cut
into 2cm pieces

25g flaked almonds

Preheat the oven to 180°C/fan 160°C/gas 4. Grease a 23cm springform or loose-bottomed cake tin and line with baking parchment.

Cream the butter with 175g of the sugar in a bowl until light and fluffy, then gradually beat in the eggs. Fold in the flour, orange zest and ground almonds and stir well until smooth and creamy.

Turn the mixture into the tin and level the surface. Scatter with the rhubarb and sprinkle over the remaining 50g sugar and the flaked almonds.

Bake for approximately 1 hour, until risen and just firm to the touch. A skewer inserted into the centre of the cake should come out with a few moist crumbs clinging to it.

Remove from the oven and leave to cool in the tin for 30 minutes before turning out on to a wire rack to cool. Serve with a dollop of crème fraiche.

This recipe also works well with gooseberries when they are in season; just replace the rhubarb with the same weight of topped and tailed gooseberries.

Norfolk beetroot & ginger passion cake

Louisa Kiddell opened the Norfolk Gluten Free shop at Hellesdon Barns on the outskirts of Norwich in 2014 to be a one-stop shop crammed full of every imaginable gluten-free product, whether local, small brand or big-name company. 'I love this rich, moist cake because of the gorgeous earthy taste. Its base is a passion cake using root vegetables – here beetroot – but with added depth from the sultanas, hazelnuts, dark muscovado sugar and stem ginger.'

The Norfolk Gluten Free Co.

serves 12

CAKE

225g grated raw beetroot

300ml light Norfolk rapeseed oil, plus extra for greasing

375g dark muscovado sugar

5 medium eggs, separated

3 tbsp milk

135g hazelnuts, roasted and chopped

300g gluten-free plain flour

3 tsp gluten-free baking powder

100g raisins or sultanas

30g stem ginger, drained and chopped

1½ tsp cinnamon

1 tsp vanilla extract

CANDIED BEETROOT

300g caster sugar

225ml water

2 small beets, thinly sliced

1 tbsp lemon juice

ICING

175g butter, soft

150g icing sugar, sifted

1 tsp vanilla extract

450g soft cream cheese, such as St Swithins from Norton's Dairy

This cake freezes well before being iced.

Preheat the oven to 180°C/160°C/gas 4. Lightly oil a 23cm cake tin and line with baking parchment.

Place 1 teaspoon grated beetroot in a small bowl, cover it with 2 teaspoons boiling water and set aside. This is to colour the icing later.

Whisk the oil and muscovado sugar together. Add the egg yolks and milk and beat until combined. Stir in the remaining beetroot and hazelnuts.

Sift the flour and baking powder together and fold into the mixture along with the fruit, ginger, cinnamon and vanilla.

Whisk the egg whites, in a clean bowl, until stiff peak stage and carefully fold into the cake mixture. Transfer to the cake tin and bake for about 1 hour and 20 minutes until the top feels springy and a skewer inserted into the centre comes out clean. Leave in the tin and cool on a wire rack.

For the candied beetroot, stir the sugar and water in a small pan over a medium heat until the sugar has dissolved, then bring to the boil. Add the beetroot, bring back to the boil, then reduce the heat to a simmer and cook for about 20 minutes or until the beetroot has become translucent and the syrup thickened. Remove the beetroot slices from the syrup and leave to cool on a baking sheet lined with baking parchment. Reserve 200ml of the syrup, add the lemon juice and set aside to cool.

For the icing, cream together the butter and icing sugar. Add the vanilla and cream cheese and mix well to combine, then add the pink water. Mix with a wooden spoon until no streaks are left.

Once the cake is completely cool, slice through the middle horizontally and sandwich the two halves together with pink icing. Cover the top of the cake with the rest of the pink icing, decorate with the candied beetroot and drizzle with the coloured syrup.

Carrot & pineapple cake

Alfred G. Pearce is a second-generation family owned business, now run by brothers Simon and Jonathan. Established in 1959 to service the needs of the canning industry, the company has developed into a fully integrated operation involved in growing, processing and marketing vegetables for food manufacturers in the UK and throughout Europe. Alfred G. Pearce supplies a wide range of prepared produce, principally root vegetables, to many of the biggest and most respected names in the food manufacturing industry.

Alfred G. Pearce

serves 10

CAKE

1 large egg and 1 egg yolk

160g plain flour

½ tsp cinnamon

¼ tsp ground cloves

½ tsp bicarbonate of soda

½ tsp baking powder

250g unrefined caster sugar

200g sunflower oil
    or a light-flavoured rapeseed oil

150g carrot, finely grated

50g desiccated coconut

70g tinned pineapple in juice,
    drained and finely chopped

2 large egg whites

Pinch salt

ICING

75g butter, soft

75g cream cheese

175g icing sugar, sifted

½ tsp vanilla extract

Preheat the oven to 180°C/160°C/gas 4. Grease the tin with a little extra oil and line the base of a 22cm wide, 6cm deep springform tin with baking parchment.

Prepare the ingredients: whisk the whole egg and egg yolk together; sift together the flour, spices, bicarbonate of soda and baking powder in a bowl.

In a food mixer, whisk the sugar and oil together for a good minute, slowly pour in the eggs, followed by the carrot, coconut and pineapple, and finally the dry ingredients.

Whisk the egg whites in a clean bowl until they form firm peaks, then gently fold them into the cake mixture, by hand, using a metal spoon, a spoonful at a time.

Pour the mixture into the prepared cake tin and bake for 50–60 minutes. To test if the cake is cooked, slide a skewer into the centre. If it comes out clean, it's ready. Once the cake is cooked, allow to cool, then remove it from the tin.

To make the icing, place all the ingredients in a bowl or food processor and beat well until a smooth creamy consistency. Once the cake is completely cooled, smooth the icing over it. Leave in a cool place so the topping sets before serving.

To add colour, garnish the cake with fine julienne strips of carrot, softened and glazed in a little hot sugar syrup.

Raspberry, orange & chocolate gateau

'Our principle at Strattons is to eat the seasons: fresh food locally produced in our garden, scrumped, traded, nurtured, foraged or simply from a producer we admire. Operating from a listed building, we are acutely aware that we are one of a series of caretakers of an historic site; it was fascinating to read in old papers found in the cellar that in 1942, the "private residence the Villa", as it was then, was designated as an emergency feeding station for the town of Swaffham in the event of invasion. It's satisfying still to be a part of its food and community connection today. With huge thanks to head chef Julia Hetherton for her recipe.'

Strattons Hotel, Swaffham

serves 10–12

JACONDE SPONGE

6 eggs, separated
250g caster sugar
125g ground almonds
125g plain flour

BUTTERCREAM

250g unsalted butter
500g icing sugar
¼ tsp pink food colour
Raspberry flavour drops, to taste

ORANGE SYRUP

1 orange, zest and juice
300g caster sugar
300ml water

GANACHE

150ml double cream
300g dark chocolate (70 per cent cocoa solids), chopped

GLAZE

150g dark chocolate
90ml double cream
2 tsp honey

DECORATION

Fresh raspberries, pink shimmer dust, chocolate transfers or chocolate decorations, pink edible glitter

Preheat the oven to 180°C/fan 160°C/gas 4. Butter and line two 45x30cm trays with baking parchment.

Make the jaconde first: whisk the egg yolks with half the sugar until pale and fluffy. In a clean bowl, whisk the egg whites with the remaining sugar until stiff.

Sift the almonds and flour together. Fold a third of whites into the yolk mix followed by a third of the dry ingredients; continue until all are combined. Divide between the trays and level with an angled palette knife. Bake for 10–12 minutes until light brown.

For the buttercream, beat the butter in an electric mixer until soft, then slowly add the icing sugar. Then, with the mixer on high, beat until creamy and smooth. Add the colour and flavour.

Put the ingredients for the orange syrup in a pan and gently bring to a simmer. Once it starts to boil, take it off the heat.

For the ganache, put the cream in a pan and bring to the boil. Remove from the heat, add the chocolate and stir until smooth.

Put the glaze ingredients in a pan and heat gently until smooth.

To assemble: line a baking tray with baking parchment. Cut each sponge in half horizontally.

Place one rectangle of sponge on the baking parchment and soak the top with orange syrup using a pastry brush. With an angled palette knife, spread an even layer of buttercream over the sponge. Place another piece of sponge on top, soak well with syrup, then spread with an even layer of ganache. Add another piece of sponge, soak again and cover with an even layer of buttercream.

Place the last piece of sponge on top, soak with a little less syrup this time and spread with a thinner layer of buttercream. Level with the palette knife. Place the cake on the tray in the fridge for 30 minutes to firm up.

▶▶

To finish, pour the chocolate glaze over the top and level with the palette knife. Put the cake back in the fridge for 30 minutes to firm up. Trim the edges of the cake to show the neat layers, then decorate, making it as fancy as you like.

When trimming the cake, use a serrated bread knife that has been warmed in a jug of hot water and then dried.

Chocolate truffle birthday cake

'This cake is probably the cake I have made the most in my life and it works well for so many occasions. Simple to make, with a wonderful flavour, rich and creamy with a little rum in the back ground. I would like to dedicate this recipe to my father-in-law, Robin Harper, who lost his life to cancer. Robin was the most gentle of gentlemen and was a real lover of all things chocolate. I made him this cake for his last birthday and decorated it with lots of chocolate garnishes.'

John 'Grimsby' Watt, Pye Bakers of Norwich

serves 12–16

CHOCOLATE SPONGE

8 medium eggs

250g caster sugar

200g plain flour

50g cocoa powder

RUM SYRUP

100ml water

60g caster sugar

25g dark rum

CHOCOLATE MOUSSE

500g dark chocolate
(70 per cent cocoa solids)

1 litre whipping cream

50g caster sugar

CHOCOLATE GLAZE

125g dark chocolate
(70 per cent cocoa solids)

90ml whipping cream

55g glucose

25ml rum

50g butter, diced

Preheat the oven to 170°C/150°C/gas 3. Butter a 28cm round springform baking tin and line with baking parchment.

For the sponge, whisk the eggs and caster sugar in an electric mixer for about 10 minutes until pale, light and fluffy.

Sift the flour and cocoa powder into the bowl, folding in with a rubber spatula as lightly as possible to avoid knocking out the air . When all the flour is mixed in, pour into the tin and bake on the middle shelf of the oven for 30 minutes. Test that the cake is ready by putting a skewer into the middle; if it comes out clean, it is ready. If not, bake the cake for another 5 minutes then recheck. When cooked, put on a wire rack to cool for 15 minutes, then remove from the tin.

For the rum syrup, put the water and sugar in a small pan and bring to the boil. When all the sugar has dissolved, then take off the heat, add the rum and set aside to cool.

For the mousse, melt the chocolate in a large glass bowl over a pan of hot water. Use a rubber spatula to stir until fully melted. Set the bowl aside.

In an electric mixer, whisk the cream and caster sugar together until thickened but not stiff. Pour a third of the cream into the chocolate and fold in until marbled. Pour this back into the bowl with the cream. Fold together until smooth and well combined. This has to be done quickly as the cold of the cream can set the chocolate.

To assemble the cake, place a 28cm wide, 4cm deep cake ring on a cake card. Cut the sponge horizontally into 4 discs. Use 2 discs for this cake and freeze the other 2 for another cake. Put 1 disc in the cake ring and brush with rum syrup until moist but not wet. Spoon in half of the chocolate mousse, pushing the

▶▶

mousse up the sides of the ring with a pallet knife, making sure there are no air pockets. Using a plate that is slightly smaller than the remaining cake disc, cut around the plate and discard the trim. Put the second smaller disc of sponge in the middle of the ring and push it down in to the mousse. Brush with rum syrup. Spoon the remaining mousse on top and use a palette knife to create a smooth flat top. Put the cake into the freezer for 2–3 hours to set or in the fridge overnight.

For the glaze, chop the chocolate into small pieces and place in a bowl. Put the cream in a pan with the glucose and rum, heat to almost boiling, then pour over the chocolate and stir with a rubber spatula until melted and smooth. Add the diced butter and stir slowly until melted. Allow to cool until it is no longer hot but still liquid.

Take the cake from the freezer and remove from the cake card. Place on a wire rack with a tray under. Pour the glaze over the top and lift one side of the wire tray up to allow the excess glaze to run off, and then the other side until the glaze covers the whole cake. Take the excess glaze from the side of the ring with a palette knife. Do not smooth the top with a palette knife as it will leave marks. Put the cake back on the cake card and place in the fridge for 5 minutes. To serve, remove the ring by warming the sides with a blowtorch. Be careful not to get it too hot as the mousse may melt.

This cake can be made 1–2 days in advance. Serve with crème fraiche and raspberry coulis.

Chocolate and almond cake

Antony Gormley is acclaimed for his sculptures, installations and public artworks that explore the relationship of the human body to space. Vicken Parsons is a painter whose works have been exhibited extensively and are held in major public collections. Antony and Vicken have a home and studios in West Norfolk. 'This is the recipe for the delicious cake our friend Filipa brings over from Porto for us, when we are lucky enough. Her mother, a wonderful cook, makes it along with little pots of jam from the most succulent Portuguese fruits. We have now mastered it for ourselves.'

Antony Gormley and Vicken Parsons

serves 12

CAKE

335g unsalted butter

225g light soft brown sugar

6 eggs, separated

300g dark chocolate
  (70 per cent cocoa solids), grated

345g ground almonds

1½ tbsp white sugar

cocoa powder, for dusting
  (optional)

TOPPING (OPTIONAL)

40g double cream

80g dark chocolate
  (70 per cent cocoa solids)

25g blanched almonds

White chocolate, melted, to drizzle

Preheat the oven to 160°/fan 140°/gas 3. Line a 24cm round cake tin with parchment paper.

Cream the butter and brown sugar until soft and well blended, then add the egg yolks one at a time, followed by the chocolate and almonds, and beat well.

In a spotlessly clean metal or glass bowl, whisk the egg whites with the white sugar – this helps stabilize the whites – until soft peaks form, then slowly fold into the chocolate mixture. Pour into the prepared tin and gently level the top.

Bake for around 65 minutes or until a skewer comes out clean. Cool in the tin on a wire rack.

This can can be served plain, dusted with cocoa, or with a ganache topping.

To make the ganache, heat the cream in a pan over a medium heat until it boils.

Add the chocolate and remove from the heat. Stir until all the chocolate is melted and the mixture is smooth. Let the ganache stand at room temperature, stirring occasionally, for about 15 minutes, or until it begins to thicken.

Once the cake is cold, remove from the tin. Spread with ganache topping, drizzle with the melted white chocolate and scatter with blanched almonds.

This is a wonderful chocolaty moist cake, which is also gluten free. Delicious with or without the ganache topping.

Celebration fruit cake

'I first tasted this delicious cake thirty years ago at the christening of my godson, Ben Eayrs, when it had been made by a stalwart of the family, Mrs. P. I have used the recipe for every Christmas cake since, as well as for grandchildren's christening cakes, our daughter's wedding cake, sustenance on charity bike rides or just as a good traditional fruit cake that will keep well. I always use eggs from my own hens, but for all the occasion cakes the most important ingredient is love.'

Melinda Raker, Marie Curie Norfolk Patron

makes 1 large

600g currants
900g sultanas
250g glacé cherries
250g shredded peel
2 tbsp brandy
750g plain flour
Pinch salt
1 tsp bicarbonate of soda
½ tsp ground cloves
1 tsp ground cinnamon
1 tsp mixed spice
500g butter, soft
500g soft dark brown sugar
10 medium eggs
½ tsp vanilla extract
1 lemon, zest and juice
125g chopped mixed nuts
Milk, to mix

To make a nut-free version, replace the nuts with an additional 125g mixed fruit.

Two days before you bake the cake, wash then steam all the dried fruit in a large colander over a pan of simmering water for an hour, turning the fruit from time to time. This process makes the fruit swell. Leave to cool in a large bowl. When cool, pour the brandy over the fruit and leave covered in a cool place.

Preheat the oven to 150°C/fan 130°C/gas 2. Line a 28cm or 30cm cake tin with a double layer of greased baking parchment.

Sift together the flour, salt, bicarbonate of soda and spices in a large bowl.

Cream the butter and sugar together in a very large bowl with an electric hand whisk until light and fluffy. This is one of the most important elements so don't cut corners. Next, beat the eggs and add a tablespoon at a time, beating thoroughly after each addition. If it starts to look like it might curdle, add a tablespoon of the spiced flour. Then add the vanilla.

Fold in the spiced flour. Stir in the soaked fruit, lemon zest and juice, nuts and finally the milk, if necessary, to give a dropping consistency.

Pour the mix into the lined cake tin, smooth the top with a spatula, and bake for 4 hours. Insert a skewer to test the cake. If it comes out clean, the cake is cooked; if not, cook for up to another hour and test again at 15-minute intervals. When the cake is nicely browned, cover with baking parchment for the remainder of the cooking time.

Only remove from the tin when cake is completely cold. Wrap in baking parchment and then foil – if not using immediately. It will keep in this way for several weeks before marzipanning and icing, if for a special occasion.

Berries & cream celebration cake

'Anyone in the family who had a birthday in the summer months was always treated to my mother's amazing sponge cakes filled with fresh strawberries and whipped cream. They would bring a smile to the face of every recipient. This elegant buttermilk sponge, flavoured with orange and vanilla, is the one I make as I continue this special family birthday tradition.'

Mary Kemp

serves 12

CAKE

A little butter and oil for preparing
  the tin
225g self-raising flour
¼ tsp salt
1½ tsp baking powder
125ml buttermilk
1 tsp vanilla extract
125g butter, soft
275g caster sugar
2 large whole eggs
3 large egg yolks
2 oranges, zest
80ml light rapeseed or olive oil

FILLING

350ml double cream
600g mixed fresh Norfolk
  strawberries and raspberries

TO FINISH

Mint leaves

*To make a real show-stopper,
bake two of the sponges
and serve them sandwiched
together with lots of whipped
cream and fruit.*

Preheat the oven to 180°C/160°/gas 5. Lightly butter and oil a 23cm loose-bottomed cake tin and line with baking parchment.

Sift the flour, salt and baking powder into a mixing bowl. Mix together the buttermilk and the vanilla extract in a jug.

Using an electric whisk, cream the butter until light and fluffy. Add the sugar while the machine is still running slowly and mix for a good 3 minutes.

Add the whole eggs, then the egg yolks one at a time, beating for a few moments before adding the next.

Stir in the orange zest and oil by hand and mix well. Once combined, fold in half the flour, followed by half the buttermilk mixture, stirring well. Then add the rest of the flour, and finally the remaining buttermilk. Pour the batter into the prepared cake tin.

Bake for approximately 30 minutes, until the cake is firm and the edges are starting to come away from the sides of the tin. If the cake starts to brown too quickly, turn the heat down slightly. Once cooked, cool the cake in the tin for 15 minutes, then turn out on to a wire rack.

Whip the cream and slice the berries, reserving the best berries for the top. Split the sponge in half and fill with cream and sliced berries. Garnish with berries and mint leaves.

Plum & almond cake

'Barsby Produce is a small, independent business that has been serving the East Anglian region with top quality fresh produce for over forty years. We source and supply a range of fresh goods, including fruit, vegetables, dairy and fine foods. More recently Barsby has been working tirelessly to shorten and relocalise our supply chain to strengthen the link between primary producer and end-user. Through long-term relationships and working collaboratively, we source vegetables from the agriculturally rich farmlands of Norfolk and Lincolnshire.'

Barsby Produce

serves 12, gluten free

1 lemon, roughly chopped
225g butter
225g caster sugar
3 medium eggs
200g ground almonds
115g polenta
1 tsp gluten-free baking powder
10 plums, stoned and halved
15g Demerara sugar
15g flaked almonds
Icing sugar, to dust

Preheat the oven to 180°C/fan 160°C/gas 4. Lightly grease and line a 26cm wide, 6cm deep springform tin with baking parchment.

Put the lemon pieces in a processor using the chopping blade attachment and process until finely chopped. Then add the butter and caster sugar and process again until well mixed. Add the eggs one at a time and process, followed by the ground almonds, polenta and baking powder, then process again until mixed evenly.

Spread half the mixture evenly into the prepared tin, then arrange half the plums over this, followed by the remaining cake mixture. Place the rest of the plums cut-side up over the top and sprinkle with the Demerara sugar.

Bake for 1 hour, then reduce the heat to 160°C/fan 140°C/gas 3 and sprinkle the almonds on top. Bake for a further 15 minutes until a skewer inserted into the centre of the cake comes out clean.

Serve dusted with icing sugar; lovely served warm or at room temperature with a generous dollop of crème fraiche.

This is a good all-year-round cake as it works with so many kinds of fruits, such as raspberries, blueberries, blackberries, blackcurrants, gooseberries and rhubarb.

Caramelised white chocolate & vanilla cheesecake

Ben Handley has been cooking in Norfolk for a formidable twenty-five years. He takes a local and global approach to his work after a formative time spent cooking in the cool quarter of Melbourne, Australia. Ben combines an exciting love of flavours with a keen eye on seasonality and the finest produce available in Norfolk. The Duck is a family-run country pub. It is an airy blend of contemporary and traditional design, with two wood-burning stoves for the winter months. The pretty garden sits beneath a canopy of mature apple trees and attracts Stanhoe's local duck residents during the summer, a sweet English spectacle.

Ben Handley, chef/patron, The Duck Inn, Stanhoe

serves 8–10

BASE
200g digestive biscuits
200g ginger nut biscuits
200g unsalted butter melted

FILLING
150g white chocolate drops
400g soft cream cheese
300g caster sugar
1 lemon, zest and juice
300ml double cream
1 vanilla pod, split in half and seeds
    extracted with the point of a knife

CRANBERRY AND ALMOND SALSA
70g almonds, chopped and toasted
6 tbsp runny honey
100g dried cranberries

Preheat the oven to 165°C/fan 145°C/gas 3. Line a 22cm non-stick springform tin with baking parchment.

In a food processor, blitz the biscuits to a fine crumb and add the melted butter until combined. Press the crumb mix into the base of the tin and pack down firmly. Bake for 10–15 minutes to firm up. Allow to cool then chill in the fridge until firm.

Meanwhile, line a large baking sheet with baking parchment. Spread the white chocolate drops evenly on to the baking parchment and bake until they have melted and slightly caramelised to a nice golden colour, checking and stirring every 5 minutes. Set aside to cool.

In a food mixer, beat the cream cheese, sugar, cooled caramelised white chocolate, lemon zest and juice until smooth.

In a separate bowl, whisk the cream and vanilla seeds until stiff peaks form. Gently fold the whipped cream into the cream cheese mixture until it is fully combined; be careful not to overwork it. Spoon on to the chilled biscuit base and, using a warm palette knife, smooth the top of the cheesecake. Chill overnight until set.

For the salsa, warm the nuts, honey and cranberries in a pan. Set aside until ready to serve.

Use a warm knife to slice the cheesecake, then spoon over the salsa.

Here we have served the cheesecake with quenelles of crème fraîche, pieces of honeycomb (see page 89 for the recipe) and sprigs of micro lemon balm.

Celebration cheesecake

'Place UK are based in Tunstead on the edge of the Norfolk Broads. A family business established in 1954 and now second generation, we are recognised as one of the UK's leading growers and processors of high quality soft fruit; you can purchase our fruit in all of the major supermarkets. Additionally, Place UK process local and imported foodstuffs – from fruit and vegetables to beans and pulses. Over the last sixty years Place UK has built an enviable reputation for quality and reliability, and for creating delicious flavour in our rapidly expanding food supply chain – naturally.'

Tim Place, Place UK Ltd

serves 12

CHEESECAKE

200g biscotti or cantuccini biscuits

100g butter

300g white chocolate

600g cream cheese

300ml double cream

50g caster sugar

1 vanilla pod, split in half and seeds extracted with the point of a knife

300g fresh summer berries

2 tbsp strawberry or other summer fruit jam

COULIS

200g mixed summer berries

1 tbsp icing sugar

3 tbsp lemon juice

Half a lemon, zest

200g mixed berries and mint, to decorate

Make this in the winter months using frozen berries.

Line the base and sides of a 22cm loose-bottomed cake tin with baking parchment.

Break up the biscuits: place them in a strong plastic bag and crush them using a rolling pin. Place the crumbs in a bowl. Melt the butter in the microwave for 1 minute, pour over the broken biscuits and stir well to combine. Push the biscuits into the bottom of the tin and level with the back of a spoon. Place in the fridge to chill while you prepare the filling.

Break the chocolate into a glass bowl; put it over a pan of just simmering water, making sure the bottom of the bowl doesn't touch the water. Stir occasionally to melt the chocolate. Set aside to cool.

Whisk the cream cheese, cream, caster sugar and vanilla seeds together using an electric whisk until thick and creamy. Stir the cheese mixture into the almost cool white chocolate until well combined.

Mix the fresh summer berries with the jam. Spoon half of the cheese mixture on top of the biscuit base. Make a layer of the jam and fruit mixture, without going all the way to the edge. Spoon the remaining cheese mixture on top, and level it off. Cover and chill for 6 hours or overnight.

To make the fruit coulis, blitz the fruit with the sugar and lemon juice, pass through a sieve, then add the lemon zest.

Loosen the tin, remove the cheesecake and discard the paper liner. Spoon a little of the fruit coulis on to the cheesecake and top with the summer berries; serve the remainder of the coulis separately.

Linzertorte

'The Linzertorte has been around for centuries – I sometimes feel as if I have been too, but generally only after a 17-hour stint at The Lavender House stove. In truth, the Linzertorte is just a glorified jam tart, but what a tart it is: incredibly short, crumbly almond pastry and the best jam you have (I choose strawberry, it reminds me of my mum's kitchen). It's a favourite in the baking classes at The Richard Hughes Cookery School.'

Richard Hughes, The Lavender House, Brundall

serves 6–8

175g plain flour

1 tsp powdered cinnamon

Pinch ground cloves

1 lemon, zest

175g ground almonds

40g caster sugar

175g butter, cut into 1.5cm pieces and chilled

1 medium egg yolk

400g homemade or good quality strawberry jam

Icing sugar, to dust

Preheat the oven to 200°C/180°C fan/gas 6. Butter a 20–23cm loose-bottomed flan dish or a deep plate.

Sift the flour into a large bowl with the cinnamon and cloves. Add the lemon zest, ground almonds and sugar, then rub in the butter by hand. Once the mixture resembles breadcrumbs, gently mix in the egg yolk to form a soft dough. Chill for a good 15–20 minutes.

Roll out two-thirds of the pastry between two sheets of greaseproof paper. The pastry is very short and the paper will help you both to roll it and to transfer it to the flan dish. Line the flan dish with the pastry and patch it if you need to. A useful tip is to dampen your hands slightly with water, which prevents the dough sticking to them.

Spread the jam evenly over the pastry.

Roll out the remaining pastry and cut into strips long enough to cover the tart. Lay the strips across the top of the jam filling to create a lattice pattern.

Chill for another 20 minutes.

Bake the Linzertorte for 30–40 minutes until the pastry is deep golden brown. Dust with icing sugar.

Jammy coconut tarts

'I was born in Croxton near Thetford in 1912, one of twelve, six boys and six girls – I was the eleventh. My father was a warrener and had rabbit to eat every day of his life, including Christmas Day. My mother was a wonderful woman and worked very, very hard. She always made sure we had good hot meals and warm clothes to wear. I went into domestic service at fourteen and I married my husband Fred at twenty-one. I was baptised, confirmed and married in Croxton Church. I cooked meals for me and my sister Iris until a month before my hundredth birthday.'

Alice Syzling

This recipe has been sponsored by Wayland Free Range Eggs. 'We produce healthy and nutritious free-range eggs on our family-run farms. Our hens must be happy, because they lay extremely tasty eggs.'
Peter Ewin

makes 12

PASTRY
115g plain flour
55g butter, cubed
1 medium egg yolk, beaten
I scant dessertspoon cold water

FILLING
50g unsalted butter
40g caster sugar
½ tsp vanilla extract
1 medium egg
130g desiccated coconut
20g plain flour
¼ tsp baking powder

Preheat the oven to 180°C/fan 160°C/gas 4.

Butter a 12-hole tart tray.

To make the pastry, combine the flour and butter in a food processor and process until the mixture resembles breadcrumbs. Add the beaten egg yolk and pulse, adding enough cold water for the dough to form a ball. Gently knead then wrap in cling film and chill for 20 minutes.

To make the filling, cream the butter, sugar and vanilla extract with an electric whisk, then add the egg. Finally fold in the coconut, flour and baking powder with a wooden spoon.

Roll out the pastry and, using a cutter or a teacup, cut out circles slightly bigger than the holes in the tart tray (about 6cm). Press a circle of pastry into each hole, spread a teaspoon of jam into each tart, then divide the filling between them. With the pastry offcuts, make a cross for the tops. Bake for 18–20 minutes until golden, then remove the little tarts from their tins and cook on a baking tray for a further 3–4 minutes to crisp the pastry. Best served warm.

This recipe comes with memories of baking with Mother, helping fill the tarts with jam and making the crosses to go on top.

Praline tart

Byfords started in September 2000 with a low-key café located in one of Holt's most historic buildings. It has developed into an all-day café, shop and posh bed and breakfast with a self-catering apartment. Believed to be the town's oldest building, this beautiful, Grade-II listed property has a wealth of character. A visit to this friendly, family-run concern is about the whole experience – beautiful building, superb location, wonderful food, all mixed with an easy-going attitude and ready smile.

Byfords, Holt

serves 8–10

PASTRY

250g plain flour, plus extra
    for dusting

Pinch salt

125g butter, cold, plus extra
    for greasing

3 medium egg yolks

125g caster sugar

Cold water, to bind

FILLING

600ml double cream

3 drops vanilla extract

150g caster sugar

600g dark chocolate (70 per cent
    cocoa solids)

75g butter

225g whole roasted hazelnuts,
    roughly crushed

Fresh raspberries, to serve (optional)

*For a sweet-and-salt variation,
use salted roasted pecans
and drizzle with caramel.*

Lightly butter a 25cm fluted flan tin.

To make the pastry, place the flour, salt and butter into a bowl and rub between your fingers until the mixture resembles breadcrumbs. Add the egg yolks and sugar and knead until the mixture comes together to form a dough; add a dash of cold water if you need a little extra liquid to bind the pastry. Put in a bowl, cover the bowl with cling film and chill in the fridge for 30 minutes.

Preheat the oven to 200°C/fan 180°C/gas 6.

Roll the pastry out on a lightly floured surface and ease into the tin, then place a piece of baking parchment on top and weigh it down with baking beans or rice. Bake in the oven for 15 minutes, then remove the paper and beans and return to the oven for 10 minutes, or until lightly browned.

For the filling, bring the cream, vanilla extract and sugar slowly to the boil in a pan.

Break the chocolate and cut the butter into small pieces and place in a large bowl. Pour the hot cream mixture over the chocolate and butter and whisk slowly until the chocolate has melted and the mixture is smooth.

Sprinkle three-quarters of the hazelnuts into the cooked case and pour the chocolate mixture over. Scatter the remaining nuts on the top and leave to cool in the fridge for 2 hours to set. Serve with fresh raspberries piled on top, if you like.

Norfolk Tart

'Moving from a career in medicine to one in food has been an extraordinary experience. The business has grown from selling cakes at farmers' markets to opening a patisserie in Norwich city centre. That journey would always have been amazing but to do it in the county I love surrounded and supported by its good folk has been very special. A contemporary take on a traditional Norfolk recipe, this tart is flavoured with rich sugars, syrup and fragrant honey. The salt and milk powder balance the sweetness, adding a modern twist to a dish that Charles Dickens is said to have enjoyed.'

Tim Kinnaird, Macarons & More

serves 10

PASTRY

100g unsalted butter, plus extra
    for greasing
65g icing sugar, plus extra
    for dusting the finished tart
1 vanilla pod
20g ground almonds
1 small egg, beaten
175g plain flour, plus extra
    for dusting

FILLING

160g soft light brown sugar
160g caster sugar
80g honey
80g golden syrup
1 scant tsp salt
3 tbsp milk powder
250g unsalted butter, melted
150g double cream
8 medium egg yolks

*Serve with vanilla ice cream
or a dollop of extra thick cream.*

Lightly butter and flour a 26cm tart ring or case.

Cream the butter and icing sugar until fluffy and pale. Split the vanilla pod and scrape the seeds into the bowl, stirring well. Mix in the ground almonds, then gradually add the egg until fully incorporated. Fold in the flour. Bring the mixture together and knead briefly, then cover in cling film and chill until firm – at least 1 hour.

Roll out on a lightly floured surface until 2–3mm thick and line the tart case. Trim the pastry slightly but leave it overhanging the edge of the case as you'll achieve a neater finish if it's finally trimmed after baking. Chill for another hour; this helps prevent the pastry shrinking when baked.

Preheat the oven to 170°C/fan 150°C/gas 3.

Line the pastry case with parchment paper and baking beans and blind-bake for 15–20 minutes. The case needs to be set and a light brown colour on the base. Remove the baking paper and beans and set the case aside.

When making the filling, it's important to incorporate as little air as possible; air causes the mix to soufflé up and over the edge. Mix together the sugars, honey, syrup, salt and milk powder. Mix in the melted butter, then the double cream. As gently as possible, stir the egg yolks through until it's all well combined.

Pour the mixture into the pastry case and bake for 30–35 minutes until brown on top and set around the edge. The centre should still be a little wobbly as the residual heat in the tart will continue to cook the mixture out of the oven. Allow to cool and then dust with icing sugar.

Raspberry Bakewell tart

The Ingham Swan is a fourteenth-century thatched former coaching inn, an award-winning restaurant-with-rooms offering fine dining in relaxed surroundings close to the Broads and the stunning Norfolk coastline, run by Chef/Patron Daniel Smith and his team. Daniel bought The Ingham Swan with old school friend and business partner Gregory Adjemian. Now the 50-seat Ingham Swan is featured in the Michelin Guide, Good Pub Guide and Alastair Sawday's Pubs & Inns of England & Wales, and has held a coveted Michelin Bib Gourmand for three years. The Ingham Swan is about serving good, honest, reasonably priced food with a menu dedicated to seasonality and the freshest local ingredients.

The Ingham Swan

serves 12

PASTRY

320g plain flour, sifted, plus extra
    for dusting

25g sugar

180g butter, diced

½ vanilla pod

1 medium egg yolk

6 tbsp raspberry conserve

FRANGIPANE

250g unsalted butter, soft

250g sugar

50g flour

250g ground almonds

5 medium eggs

180g fresh raspberries

Flaked almonds, for sprinkling

Preheat the oven to 180°C/fan 160°C/gas 4. Butter a 23cm wide, 5cm deep loose-bottomed flan case.

Rub the flour, sugar and butter together until breadcrumb consistency. Add the seeds from the vanilla pod and the egg yolk and bring together to form a dough. Wrap in cling film and refrigerate for at least 45 minutes.

Roll out the pastry on a lightly floured board to 3mm thickness. Use to line the tart tin, then trim and chill for 15 minutes.

Spread the raspberry conserve on the pastry case base, leaving a 1cm gap around the edge, and chill for another 15 minutes.

For the frangipane, beat together the butter and sugar. Fold in the flour and ground almonds and mix in the eggs to give smooth consistency. Pour into the pastry case. Bake for 20 minutes, then remove from the oven, stud with the raspberries and sprinkle with flaked almonds. Cover with baking parchment with a hole in the middle for the steam to escape and to prevent the top catching. Bake for a further 20–30 minutes until golden brown.

Eat at room temperature.

A blackberry Bakewell tart would be lovely in the autumn months, especially served with custard

Norfolk strawberry & mint flan with clotted cream

The Maids Head Hotel is known to be the oldest hotel in the UK and has been offering hospitality to its guests for over 800 years. Situated in the historical centre of Norwich, this independent hotel has charm and individual character. The Wine Press restaurant offers simply prepared, delicious, comforting food, sourced from local suppliers. It was first awarded its one rosette back in 2008 and went on to win the EDP Best Food & Drink experience five years later. The restaurant offers 45 wines by the glass: an opportunity to savour expensive and rare wines in affordable portions.

Maids Head Hotel, Norwich

serves 12

SPONGE FLAN
4 medium eggs
100g caster sugar
100g plain flour

TOPPING
100ml water
40g fresh mint
40g caster sugar
Half a lemon, juice
4g leaf gelatine
250g clotted cream
600g fresh strawberries
Whole fresh strawberries and mint
  leaves, to serve (optional)

Preheat the oven to 160°C/fan 140°C/gas 3. Grease a 30cm sponge flan mould and line the raised centre with baking parchment.

Break the eggs into a bowl and add the sugar. Whisk with a hand-held electric whisk until thick. Sift the flour over the surface of the mixture and fold in gently with a metal spoon. Turn into the prepared mould.

Bake for 20 minutes until the sponge has risen and is golden. The centre should spring back when lightly pressed. Allow to cool slightly, then trim the edges, if the sponge has risen over the sides. Turn out on to a wire rack. Remove the paper and leave to cool.

For the topping, pour the water over half the fresh mint and blitz with a hand blender. Pour into a saucepan, add the sugar and lemon juice, then slowly cook over a low heat for 5 minutes until all sugar is dissolved. Strain.

Soak the gelatine in cold water. When it is soft, squeeze out the liquid and add to the mint solution. Whisk together then leave to cool. Chop the remaining mint finely and add to the jelly.

To assemble the flan, smooth the clotted cream on to the flan base. Cut the strawberries into slices and arrange on top. Pour the cooled mint syrup mixture over the strawberries and place in the fridge for at least 45 minutes for the mint jelly to set. Serve with whole strawberries and mint leaves piled on top, if you like.

English Whisky mince pies

'St Georges Distillery was founded in 2006 in the heart of Norfolk, near East Harling, by the Nesltrop family. Why England, and why Roudham, Norfolk? Well, there are only two main ingredients in whisky and we have them both. We have the cleanest water from our Breckland aquifer borehole, and we have the barley as Norfolk is one of the world's premier growing regions. Our whisky is batch-made by hand, left to sleep in casks until our distillers consider it perfect, then bottled by hand – one bottle at a time. We believe you will taste the difference.'

English Whisky Co.

makes 8 x 250g jars mincemeat and 18 large or 36 small pies

ENGLISH WHISKY
MINCEMEAT

240g raisins

160g sultanas

160g currants

50g mixed peel

50g ready-to-eat prunes, chopped

240g soft dark brown sugar

160g beef suet or shredded
  vegetable suet

450g grated cooking apple

2 oranges and 2 lemons,
  zest and juice

50g flaked almonds, chopped

50g hazelnuts (or add more
  currants), chopped

4 tsp ground mixed spice

2 tsp freshly grated nutmeg

120ml Chapter 6 English Whisky

MINCE PIES

230g plain flour

130g unsalted butter, chilled
  and diced

1 orange, zest

70g icing sugar, plus extra
  for dusting

1 small egg yolk

A drop of milk

1 egg, beaten with a pinch of salt,
  to glaze

1 jar homemade English Whisky
  mincemeat

Place all the ingredients for the mincemeat except the whisky in a large bowl and mix well. Cover in cling film and stand somewhere cool overnight.

The next morning preheat the oven to 120°C/fan 100°C/gas ½.

Pour the mincemeat into a large roasting tin, cover with foil and cook for about hours. The apples and suet will soften and the colour will darken. Remove the tin from the oven, allow to cool, then add the whisky, stirring well. Spoon the mixture into sterilised jars and store somewhere cool.

For the pies, quickly blitz the flour and butter in a food processor. Add the zest and sugar and give it another quick burst. Next add the egg yolk and a little milk to bind the dough. Wrap in cling film and chill in the fridge for at least an hour.

Preheat the oven to 200°C/fan 180°/gas 6. Butter an 18-hole bun tin or 36-hole mini muffin tray.

Roll out the pastry thinly on a lightly floured surface. Cut out discs to fit your chosen tin using a fluted-edge cutter and line each hole with the pastry. Generously fill each case with 1 teaspoon mincemeat if small, 2 if large.

Roll out the pastry trimmings and cut out a smaller disc to cover each pie, or use a star cutter. Brush the tops with egg glaze and bake until golden brown: small pies for 10 minutes or larger pies for 15. Dust with icing sugar to serve.

Lovely served with English whisky butter: cream 150g butter with 225g icing sugar, 50g ground almonds and 3 tbsp Chapter 6 English Whisky, then chill.

Peanut butter parfait

'I love a pud, although much to the annoyance of my wife Victoria and children, Sophie and Joe, I often don't order one when we're out but prefer to "sample" from all of theirs. We have many favourites at The Mulberry Tree, which has made it quite difficult to decide which one to share with you. Thanks to our head chef, Haydn, for handing over the recipe. Hopefully you will try it and enjoy it as much as we and our customers do. If you master the honeycomb, you'll never look back.'

Phil Milligan, The Mulberry Tree, Attleborough

makes 1kg

PARFAIT
1 x 395g tin condensed milk
200g peanut butter
1 vanilla pod, split in half and seeds extracted with the point of a knife
500ml double cream

HONEYCOMB
100g caster sugar
50g honey
1 dessertspoon liquid glucose
25g bicarbonate of soda

Serve sandwiched in wafers as a family treat.

Line a 900g loaf tin with baking parchment or cling film.

Put the unopened tin of condensed milk into a pan, cover with water and boil for 3 hours, checking and topping up the water regularly. Allow to cool completely, then open and spoon the resulting toffee and into a bowl. Add the peanut butter and vanilla, with 2 tbsp of the cream to loosen the mix, and beat using an electric whisk.

In a separate bowl, fully whip the double cream.

Fold together the cream and peanut toffee mixture using a spatula. Don't whisk as this will knock the air out. Pour the mixture into the loaf tin and freeze for 24 hours. Once frozen, this can be taken from the container and sliced. Allow a few minutes before serving to soften it slightly. Serve with the honeycomb on the side.

For the honeycomb, first line a frying pan with baking parchment. Gently heat the sugar, honey and glucose and, using a digital temperature probe, take to 155°C. Remove from the heat and add the bicarbonate of soda, whisking until all the powder has dissolved, then pour out on to the greaseproof paper and allow to cool completely. Break up and store in a Kilner jar.

Strawberry & black pepper ice cream with shortbread

'I still remember from my childhood the anticipation and the thrill of the first strawberries of the year – English, of course. There were no imported strawberries in those days. The strawberries had a wonderful, rich, bright red bloom on them and we smothered them with sugar and rich cream. Here we have the fruit and the cream combined with the added twist of a good grinding of black pepper – it really does bring out the flavour. Indulge your guests, or indeed just yourself, with this "taste of summer" ice cream in pretty dishes with spoons and shortbread biscuits on the side.'

Neil Alston

serves 6

ICE CREAM

450g really ripe English strawberries, hulled weight

300ml double cream

150g caster sugar

½ lemon, juiced

15–20 black peppercorns, freshly ground

SHORTBREAD BISCUITS

175g plain flour

85g semolina

75g caster sugar, plus extra for dusting

175g unsalted butter, diced

For the ice cream, blitz the strawberries, cream and sugar in a food processor. Add the lemon juice and black pepper to taste and blitz well again. Pass through a sieve (you still get a peppery flavour even though you lose some of the ground corns here), then churn in an ice-cream maker for a good 40–50 minutes. Store in an airtight container in the freezer.

For the shortbread, preheat the oven to 160C°/fan 140°C/gas 3. Line a large baking sheet with baking parchment.

Mix the flour and semolina in a bowl, add the sugar and butter and, using your fingertips, rub until the mixture just starts to bind. Knead lightly until it forms a smooth dough. Transfer to a work surface that has been dusted with caster sugar.

Roll the dough out to a thickness of about 1cm. Cut into rounds using a fluted biscuit cutter. Place on the baking sheet and bake in the centre of the oven for 35–40 minutes until a very pale golden brown.

Remove from the oven, dust generously with caster sugar and leave to cool on the baking tray for 5 minutes. Carefully remove to a wire rack to cool completely and then store in a tin.

If you don't have an ice-cream maker, blitz the strawberries, sugar, lemon juice and black pepper, then pass through a sieve. Whip the double cream until soft peaks form, fold into the strawberry juice, then freeze for 24 hours.

Raspberry & passion fruit Swiss roll

CoCoes, named after the Coe family who had printed on the site for four generations, was opened in answer to the constant question: 'Where can I buy the local ingredients/products you use in the hotel?' The café/deli open-plan kitchen is a place where the chefs cook and customers engage and talk about recipes, produce, life and, in time-honoured tradition, politics. The Swiss roll did not originate in Switzerland and is almost certainly a nineteenth-century creation and something of a British classic. Traditionally it's a whisked fatless sponge rolled with fruits, jams, fruit curds, cream, soft cheese . . . the possibilities are endless.

CoCoes, Strattons Hotel, Swaffham

serves 8

SWISS ROLL

2 medium eggs

1 medium egg white

125g caster sugar, plus extra for sprinkling

1 tsp vanilla paste

100g self-raising flour

FILLING

2 tbsp icing sugar

200g smooth ricotta cheese

75ml double cream, whipped until just thick

1 tsp vanilla extract

300g raspberries

4 passion fruit

Preheat the oven to 200°C/fan 180°C/gas 6. Lightly grease a 23x33cm shallow Swiss roll tin and line the base with baking parchment, leaving the paper hanging over the two long sides.

Using a food mixer or electric whisk, beat the eggs, egg white, sugar and vanilla paste in a large bowl on high speed for 5 minutes until light and foamy. Sift the flour into the bowl and fold in quickly and lightly.

Pour the mixture into the prepared tin and evenly smooth the surface. Bake for 8–10 minutes, or until the sponge springs back when lightly touched – do not be tempted to overcook as this will create cracks in the cake when rolled. Lay a sheet of baking paper on a tea towel and sprinkle lightly with caster sugar.

Turn the sponge out on to the sugared paper, remove the lining paper and, starting from a short end, roll up the sponge with the paper, using the tea towel as a guide. Cool for 30 minutes.

Sift the icing sugar into a bowl with the ricotta, double cream and vanilla, then mix together with a wooden spoon. Unroll the sponge and spread with the ricotta mixture, leaving a 2cm border at the far end. Scatter over the raspberries and pulp from the passion fruits and then carefully re-roll the sponge. Trim the ends, and cut into slices to serve.

Try rolling it with slightly softened ice-cream and jam, then freeze for a real retro pud.

Summer berry mille feuille

New Zealander Chris Coubrough has played a major role in helping North Norfolk establish itself as one of the hotspots of England's culinary revolution. The Kiwi chef worked at top restaurants in Switzerland, London and Suffolk before settling on the Saltmarsh Coast more than ten years ago. His upbringing on a remote farm on New Zealand's North Island nurtured a love of food and the outdoor life. Father-of-two Chris is the owner of the Crown Hotel in Wells-next-the-Sea and the Ship Hotel in Brancaster, and has featured in his own regional TV cookery series, Coastal Kitchen.

Chris Coubrough, The Crown At Wells next the Sea

serves **4**

PASTRY

1 sheet pre-rolled all-butter puff pastry or an all-butter puff pastry block rolled out to 30x45cm

Egg wash: 1 egg whisked with a dash of milk

Icing sugar, for dusting

PASTRY CREAM

1 vanilla pod

150ml whole milk

4 egg yolks

65g caster sugar

15g cornflour

250ml double cream, whipped

FRUIT FILLING

200g strawberries

150g raspberries

50g blackberries

50g blueberries

50ml sloe gin

Fresh mint, to garnish

Preheat the oven to 220°C/fan 200°C/gas 7. Line a baking tray with baking parchment.

Cut the pastry into 3 rectangles of 30x15cm. Place the rectangles on the baking tray and brush with egg wash. Bake for 10–12 minutes. Once the pastry rectangles have risen and cooked, pull out the paper from the tray and dust the pastry with icing sugar. Turn the oven to grill and place the pastry under the grill for 2 minutes – they will go golden brown very quickly so keep a close eye on them. Remove and cool on a cooling rack.

To prepare the pastry cream, spilt the vanilla pod and scrape the seeds into the milk. Bring the milk to the boil, then stand the pan to one side. Whisk the yolks and sugar until they become thick and creamy, then add the cornflour. Continue whisking and slowly pour in the milk. Pour the custard back into the pan and heat through, stirring until thickened. Finally pour the hot pastry cream into a clean bowl and cover the surface of the custard with cling film (to stop a skin forming). Chill in the fridge till cold and then fold in the whipped double cream.

For the fruit filling, hull or trim the fruit into a bowl and pour the sloe gin over.

Assemble just before serving. Place a pastry sheet on a serving dish, evenly spread with half the pastry cream, then add half the fruit. Top with another pastry sheet and repeat the process. Top with your best and last piece of pastry and dust with icing sugar. Garnish with fresh mint.

Cook the pastry and make the fillings ahead of time. It will then only take a few moments to create the finished mille feuille – ready to wow your guests with this wonderful taste of summer.

Strawberry & elderflower panna cotta

Norfolk Cordial sources top quality produce from local growers to create premium, pure fruit syrups for the discerning adult palate. All the ingredients are cold-pressed, which enables the syrups to retain the pure, fresh flavours of these regional fruits and flowers. When diluted, the syrups create our trademark, well-balanced, low-sugar, non-alcoholic drinks. We do not use preservatives, colourings, flavourings or concentrates – it really is that simple. This wonderful summer recipe was developed working with Nick Edgar, the joint head chef at Le Manoir aux Quat'Saisons. It looks stunning served in an elegant glass – a dessert with the wow factor.

Norfolk Cordial

serves 4

PANNA COTTA
200ml double cream
200ml milk
40g sugar
18ml elderflower cordial
6g leaf gelatine, soaked in a bowl of cold water
200g diced strawberries

STRAWBERRY JELLY
25ml water
3g leaf gelatine, soaked in a bowl of cold water
75ml strawberry and lime cordial

Serve with a homemade crunchy biscuit such as a ginger biscuit or the shortbread on page 91.

Place the cream, milk, sugar and cordial in a pan and bring it to the boil. When it comes up to the boil, whisk in the drained gelatine, then pass through a sieve.

Pour the panna cotta cream into 4 glasses, then divide the diced strawberries evenly between them. Place in the fridge and chill for 1 hour.

For the jelly, bring the water to the boil in a pan, then remove from the heat, add the drained gelatine and whisk until dissolved. Stir in the strawberry and lime cordial, then pour the jelly over the set panna cotta, dividing it evenly between the glasses. Leave in fridge to set for 20 minutes.

Strawberry & sparkling elderflower jelly

'Jellies have been the centrepiece on teatime menus for many generations. As a child jellies were part of our birthday tea treats, often with the addition of hundreds and thousands. Then at Christmas my mother would make crystal-clear red jellies, served in Victorian custard glasses to add to the festive flavours. This is one of my favourite jelly recipes.'

Mary Kemp

serves 8

500g strawberries, hulled
100g caster sugar
1 lemon, juice
8 sheets leaf gelatine
75cl bottle sparkling
    elderflower water

Slice the strawberries, place in a large heatproof bowl over a pan of simmering water and stir in the sugar and lemon juice. Cover the bowl with cling film and leave on a low heat for 30–40 minutes, checking the water level occasionally and topping it up with boiling water as necessary. Don't let the water touch the base of the bowl. The fruit will produce a clear, pink, fragrant juice.

Pour the strawberry juice into the sieve and leave it to drip through but don't be tempted to press the pulp otherwise the juice will become cloudy. Discard the fruit pulp.

Soften the gelatine sheets in cold water. Meanwhile, pour about a quarter of the strawberry juice into a clean pan and heat until just on the point of boiling, then take off the heat. Remove the gelatine from the cold water, squeezing out any excess water, and add to the hot juice, whisking until dissolved. Add back to the remaining strawberry juice.

If the liquid is still warm, allow to cool, then pour in the sparkling elderflower.

Assemble 8 cocktail or other glasses or champagne flutes. Divide the strawberry elderflower liquid equally between them and chill in the fridge until completely set.

To serve, top with a thin float of double cream or a spoonful of whipped cream. Also wonderful served with Neil Alston's Strawberry and Black Pepper Ice Cream on page 91.

savoury

Pea, ham & cheese muffins

'The wonderful soils of North and East Norfolk provide a great growing environment and, coupled with the influence of the coastal climate, produce the best-tasting peas in the world. Peas need to be frozen within two and a half hours of being picked to ensure their freshness is maintained. Some of our Norfolk peas are exported all over Europe and many of the very best quality peas end up in Italy, where demand for quality cannot be met by their home-grown peas. Peas can provide a full meal of options from soup to ice cream – they should be on every classic menu somewhere.'

Yes Peas!

makes 12

100g frozen peas

300g plain flour

1 tbsp baking powder

Pinch dry mustard powder

Sea salt and freshly ground pepper

½ tsp mixed herbs or 2 tsp fresh chives, finely chopped

1 large egg

100g Boursin cheese

200ml whole milk

50g cooked ham, diced

75g Cheddar cheese, grated

Butter for greasing

Preheat the oven to 180°C/fan 160°C/gas 4. Butter a 12-hole muffin tray.

Bring a large pan of lightly salted water to the boil and blanch the frozen peas for 2 minutes. Drain and refresh under cold running water.

Sift the flour, baking powder and dry mustard powder into a large mixing bowl and add salt, pepper and the mixed herbs or chives.

In a separate bowl, lightly beat the egg with an electric whisk and add the boursin cheese, whisking until the cheese has broken up and combined smoothly with the egg. Whisk in the milk and then, using a wooden spoon, stir in the peas and ham. Pour the wet ingredients into the dry ingredients and mix lightly and quickly to combine. Spoon the mixture into the buttered muffin tray and sprinkle the top of each muffin with grated cheese. Bake for 20 minutes or until the muffins are golden brown and firm to the touch.

Turn out on to a wire rack to cool a little, but serve while still warm.

Try making a hole in the top of the hot muffins, adding a little extra boursin cheese and letting it melt before you tuck in.

Vintage Cheddar & walnut scones

Anna and Hugo's vision when they bought The Mill in 2011 was to create a family-friendly environment where people could relax over coffee and homemade cake, enjoy a delicious lunch or indulge in a gourmet dinner. Hugo: 'My mother passed away from cancer in 2007 and one of the things we loved to do in the last months of her life was to go out for a cup of her much-loved coffee and a scone. Our baker, Claire Sullivan, has perfected this recipe exactly to our taste.'

Hugo and Anna Stevenson, The Mill Café Bar and Restaurant

makes 8

450g self-raising flour,
    plus extra for dusting
110g butter, diced
1 tsp baking powder
Generous pinch salt
1 tsp freshly ground pepper
200g strong vintage Cheddar
    cheese, grated
100g roughly chopped walnuts
1 tbsp Colman's English mustard
175ml whole milk
TOPPING
1 medium egg
Pinch salt
100g strong mature Cheddar
    cheese, grated
50g roughly chopped walnuts

Preheat the oven to 220°C/fan 200°C/gas 7. Butter a baking tray and line with baking parchment.

With your fingers, rub together the self-raising flour, butter, baking powder, salt and pepper until the mixture resembles fine crumbs. Stir in the cheese and walnuts.

In a jug, whisk together the mustard and the milk. Pour three-quarters of the liquid into the flour then, using a large spoon, bring the scone mixture together. If the mixture is too dry, add a little more milk. The mixture should not be too wet or sticky, as this will affect the rise.

Now bring the dough together with your hands and tip it on to a lightly floured worktop. Knead the dough gently into a round and flatten with the palm of your hand until it is about half an inch (1cm) thick.

Using a well-floured 6cm round cutter, gently cut out your scones. Remember not to twist. Place them on the baking tray.

Make a glaze by beating the egg and salt. With a pastry brush, glaze each scone, then top them with the cheese and walnuts.

Put them into the hot oven and immediately reduce the temperature to 200°C/fan 180°C/gas 6. Bake for 20 minutes until golden brown. You will know they are ready when a skewer comes out clean and the bottom of the scone is brown and sounds hollow when tapped.

Scones love a hot oven. Leave an inch gap between them to allow for rise and spread. Do not roll the dough – gently pat it. Scones do freeze well but are best baked and eaten fresh.

Beetroot, sage, bacon & Alpine cheese bread

'G's is a family business founded by my father, Guy Shropshire, in 1952, near Ely Cambridgeshire. It expanded into Norfolk in 1960. G's and its growers have recognised and harnessed the unique properties of the fast-growing, richly fertile black fen soils to grow a variety of consistently flavoursome salad and vegetable crops. Beetroot is just one. We now know that the beetroot's health benefits and versatility comes from its richness in vitamins, minerals and antioxidants. Today, sportsmen and women are tapping into its ability to increase stamina and endurance. But most of all it is to be savoured and enjoyed.'

Peter and Clare Shropshire, G's Fresh

makes 1 large

250ml warm water

1 tsp dried yeast

1 tsp sugar

500g strong white bread flour, plus extra for dusting

½ tsp salt

1 tsp dried sage (optional)

1 tbsp extra virgin olive oil

150g cooked fresh beetroot, cooled and puréed

5 rashers smoked streaky bacon

80g Mrs Temple's Alpine cheese, grated

Replace the bacon with 3 tablespoons pumpkin seeds for a vegetarian version.

In a jug, mix the water with the yeast and sugar. Set aside to allow the yeast to activate – after 5–10 minutes there should be a layer of foam on the surface.

Put the flour, salt, sage if using and oil in a food mixer or large bowl. Pour in the water and yeast and the puréed beetroot and knead with a dough hook for 5 minutes or by hand for 10 minutes. Set aside in a draught-free place, cover with a tea towel and leave to rise for around an hour or until it has doubled in size.

Meanwhile, cook the bacon under a hot grill until crisp. Allow to cool then cut into small pieces and set aside.

Once the dough has doubled in size, place on a floured work surface and knead it once more for a minute or two, then roll into a large rectangle. Sprinkle the bacon and cheese over the surface and roll up into a log shape, tucking the ends under.

Transfer to a baking sheet, lightly cover with a tea towel and set aside for 20 minutes to rise for a second time. Preheat the oven to 220°C/fan 200°C/gas 7.

Cook the bread for around 25 minutes. When done, the bread should sound slightly hollow when tapped on the base. Serve warm, cut into thick slices with plenty of butter.

Gluten-free cheese bread

Steve is a well-known and well-respected chef. As head of the Hotel School, part of City College Norwich, he is responsible for training chefs and hospitality professionals. There can be few professional kitchens in the county that haven't had an influence from Steve Thorpe. Recently being diagnosed with coeliac disease has given him a drive to develop recipes for customers with special dietary requirements. 'This recipe is one I have adapted following a trip to Canada, using whey powder to increase the protein level in the dough, which enables it to be moulded. For this recipe I also used an off-the-shelf bread flour mix.'

Steve Thorpe, City College Norwich

makes 4 small

410g gluten-free flour mix,
   plus extra for flouring

40g milk powder

60g whey powder

15g xanthan gum

10g yeast

5g salt

400ml water at 35°C

30g butter

Vegetable oil, for greasing

100g grated Norfolk Dapple

This bread freezes well. Pre-slice before freezing for convenience.

Sift the flour, milk powder, whey powder, xanthan gum, yeast and salt into the mixing bowl of a food processor and mix well.

Combine the water and butter in a jug.

Add the liquid to the dry ingredients, mix together to form a wet dough, then beat at medium speed for about 5 minutes. The dough should be smooth and stretchy at this stage.

Lightly oil a clean 4-litre plastic container or bowl and put the dough in it. Cover the top with oiled cling film. Place in the fridge and allow to cold-prove for 12–36 hours. It will keep for up to 4 days like this.

Turn out the dough on to a gluten-free-floured surface, add two-thirds of the cheese and knead well, distributing the cheese throughout. Divide into 4 and shape into rounds. Place these on a baking sheet lined with baking parchment. Sprinkle with the remaining cheese. Allow the bread to prove at room temperature for 1–2 hours until doubled in size.

Preheat the oven to 180°C/fan 160°C/gas 4.

Bake for 15–20 minutes until golden and glazed on top. The bread is cooked if it sounds hollow when the bottom is tapped.

Potato & rosemary soda bread

'This is a delicious recipe, created for us by the award-winning Norfolk chef Vanessa Scott to celebrate the first harvest of our Norfolk Peer new potato crop in 2014. Our lunchtime event was held in a marquee adjacent to the Norfolk Peer new potato field at Cockley Cley, where we welcomed many guests, all drawn to the idea of enjoying a potato feast alfresco and viewing the first potato harvest of the year. Our guests really enjoyed the day, particularly the Heygate Farms Potato & Rosemary Soda Bread.'

William Gribbon, farm manager at Heygate Farms

makes 1 large

250g strong white bread flour, plus extra for dusting

200g spelt flour

50g oats

1 tsp fine salt

2 tsp bicarbonate of soda

175g Norfolk Peer potatoes, cooked and well crushed

150g raisins

2 tbsp freshly chopped rosemary

100ml rapeseed oil

250ml natural yoghurt

250ml milk

Preheat the oven to 220°C/fan 200°C/gas 7. Line a baking tray with baking parchment.

In a large mixing bowl, thoroughly combine the flours, oats, salt and bicarbonate of soda. Add the potato, raisins and mix in the rosemary. Make a well in the centre.

Combine the oil, yoghurt and milk then pour into the dry ingredients. The less you handle the mixture, the lighter and tastier the loaf will be. Separate your fingers out like a fork and gently combine the ingredients. This should take no more than a minute and the mixture should only just be combined; don't worry that the mixture is extremely wet.

Put plenty of flour on to the work surface and tip the mixture out on to it. Shape the dough into a round, making sure you use plenty of flour to shape the loaf and to prevent it from sticking to your fingers and the work surface. Transfer it to the baking sheet. Bake for 35 minutes until golden brown and well risen. You can test if it's cooked by tapping the bottom. If it sounds hollow it's done, otherwise return to the oven for 5 more minutes.

This deliciously moist bread is quick and easy as it doesn't need proving. Best made by hand. It can be made with leftover mash or grated roast potatoes from Sunday lunch.

Chilli chocolate bread

Chillis Galore are Kathy and Richard, aka Wilf, who started growing chillies in Norwich over two decades ago to get some different varieties to use in their cooking. After a few years of successfully growing chillies, they created a website to share their knowledge and it has grown in popularity, with a huge following worldwide. The obvious next step was developing their own homemade chilli jellies, relishes and sauces in their kitchen. Even now, all their plants are still grown in greenhouses in the back garden where different varieties are grown annually to show and sell and use in their products.

Kathy and Wilf Thompson, Chillis Galore

makes 1 large

250ml whole milk

7g (1 sachet) fast-action dried yeast

500g bread flour, plus extra
    for dusting

60g butter

40g sugar

10g salt

25g cocoa powder

2 medium eggs, gently beaten

1 tbsp Chillis Galore Red Chilli
    Jammy Relish

200g dark chocolate buttons

1 medium egg, lightly beaten,
    to glaze

Chilli jelly is a great store-cupboard ingredient to have and gives a lovely extra dimension to soups, mayonnaise, aïoli, pâtés, pies, terrines and sauces.

Heat the milk gently in a pan until it is around body temperature. It should feel neither warm nor cold when you dip in your finger.

Rub the yeast into the flour using fingertips, then rub in the butter. Add the sugar and salt and combine thoroughly, then the cocoa powder, eggs and milk. Hold the bowl with one hand and mix the ingredients with the other for around for 2–3 minutes until a dough starts to form.

Knead on a very lightly floured work surface for around 5 minutes until the dough is smooth and elastic; don't be tempted to add extra flour or you will end up with a heavy loaf. Return the dough to the bowl, cover with a tea towel and leave to rest in a warm, draught -free space for 1–2 hours until it has doubled in size.

Transfer the dough on to a lightly floured work surface, gently flatten with a rolling pin and cover with the chilli relish and chocolate buttons. Fold the dough over on to itself and knead again for about 2 minutes until the chocolate and chilli are well combined with the dough.

Shape the dough into a large ball and place on a baking sheet lined with baking parchment. Leave to rise for 1½–2 hours until light to the touch and doubled in size.

Preheat the oven to 200°C/fan 180°C/gas 6.

Glaze the loaf with the egg and bake for 35 minutes. Watch carefully towards the end of the cooking time to avoid scorching; if necessary, cover the top with baking parchment for the last 10 minutes.

The loaf is cooked when the bottom is tapped and it sounds hollow. Leave to cool on a wire rack.

The perfect pizza

Matthew and Caroline are well known in Norfolk for their superb outside-catering operation, which includes a mobile oak-fired clay oven. Matthew says: 'There is nothing quite as delicious as the taste of a freshly baked pizza from our oak-fired clay oven, or slow-cooked rare breed pork cooked as the oven cools – the crackling is straight from heaven. The smell of the wood smoke and the hands-on skill of cooking with such a simple but fundamentally ancient piece of cooking kit tunes into our primitive instincts.' If you don't have a clay oven you can still make one of Matthew's pizzas to your own taste using wonderful Norfolk ingredients.

Matthew and Caroline Owsley-Brown, Owsley-Brown Catering Company

makes 3

BASE

325ml tepid water

7g (1 sachet) dried yeast

½ tbsp caster sugar

2 tbsp olive oil

500g strong flour

½ tsp fine salt

Semolina, for dusting

6 heaped tbsp tomato purée

SUGGESTED TOPPINGS

Norfolk Fielding Cottage soft
   goat's cheese with slices
   of cooked beetroot

Norfolk St Swithins soft cheese,
   with rocket and spicy Norfolk
   Marsh Pig chorizo

Artichoke hearts, cheese and

Fruit Pig pancetta

Put the water, yeast, sugar and olive oil in a jug and leave to stand in a warm place for 20 minutes until a light froth appears on the surface, showing the yeast is activated. Meanwhile, sift together the flour and salt into the bowl of a mixing machine.

Fit the dough hook to the mixer. Pour the water and yeast into the bowl and knead on a slow speed for 10 minutes until the dough leaves the sides of the bowl and has a soft, elastic and slightly tacky texture. (You can equally make the dough by hand.)

Put the dough into a large bowl dusted with semolina. Dust semolina on top of the dough, cover with a damp cloth and leave in a warm place for about an hour or until the dough has doubled in size. Now dust your hands in semolina and plunge them into the dough to 'knock it back' i.e. take the air back out of it. Turn the dough ball out on to a semolina-dusted surface and divide into three balls of equal size. Round each dough ball in your hand until you get a nice smooth ball. With a rolling pin, roll out each ball to form a disc turning after each roll to form a nice circular disc roughly 30cm in diameter.

Preheat the oven to 240°C/220°C/gas 9.

Spread 2 heaped tablespoons of tomato purée over the surface of each pizza, and add your topping of choice. You do not need much of each ingredient – less is more. Bake in the hot oven for 8–10 minutes until the base is golden. Serve immediately.

Use semolina as the dusting vehicle when rolling out your pizzas for added crispness. If you have dough left over, roll into small balls, bake and serve as an appetiser with garlic butter.

Leek & Binham Blue pizza bread

Breckland Organics is a family run farm, growing a range of organic vegetables for year round supply to the well-known, award winning Riverford Organics in Devon as well as to various UK packhouses. The Riverford box scheme delivers around 47,000 boxes of organic vegetables every week to homes around the UK sourced from their regional organic farms and local growers.

Riverford Organics with Breckland Organics

makes 4

INFUSED OIL

40ml olive oil, plus extra for greasing

1 garlic clove, peeled

1 bird's eye chilli, halved

BASE

300g strong white flour, plus extra
  for dusting

7g (1 sachet) dried yeast

1 tsp salt

180ml lukewarm water

1½ tbsp olive oil

TOPPING

25g butter

2 small leeks, halved lengthwise
  and thinly sliced across

30g Parmesan cheese, freshly grated

100g mozzarella cheese, grated

1½ tbsp finely chopped oregano

1½ tbsp finely chopped
  flat-leaf parsley

80g Binham Blue cheese, crumbled

Salt and freshly ground pepper

Put the olive oil, garlic and chilli in a small bowl and set aside for the flavours to infuse.

To make the dough, combine the flour, yeast and salt in a bowl, then stir in the water and oil. Turn out on to a lightly floured surface and knead for 5–8 minutes until smooth and elastic. Place in a lightly oiled bowl, cover with cling film and set aside in a warm place for 1 hour or until doubled in size.

Meanwhile, heat the butter in a small frying pan, add the leeks and cook over a low to medium heat for about 10 minutes, until soft but not coloured. Season with salt and pepper. Remove from the heat and leave to cool.

Place 2 heavy-based baking sheets in the oven and preheat it to 240°C/fan 220°C/gas 9.

Combine the Parmesan, mozzarella and herbs in a small bowl. Cut 4 sheets of baking parchment, each large enough to hold a 22cm pizza.

Divide the risen dough into 4. Dust the pieces of baking parchment with a little flour and roll out each piece of dough on the parchment, making a circle about 22cm in diameter. Brush with the flavoured oil and scatter with the cheese mixture, followed by the leeks, then the Binham. Slide the pizza, still on the paper, on to the hot baking sheet and bake for 8–10 minutes, until golden. Serve immediately. Cook the remaining pizzas in the same way.

Broccoli and Norfolk Dapple tart

'The Institute of Food Research, based at the Norwich Research Park, is a publicly funded research institute that focuses on the underlying science of food and health. One of our projects has included working with the John Innes Centre, a plant science research centre, to develop Beneforté broccoli. As well as being high in vitamins A and C, Beneforté has been naturally bred to contain two to three times more of a compound called glucoraphanin, which ongoing research suggests could help maintain cardiovascular health and reduce cancer risk cancer. Beneforté broccoli has been pioneered by Norfolk-based scientists and is now available to buy in many supermarkets nationwide.'

Institute of Food Research

serves 6–8

PASTRY

200g plain flour, plus extra
  for dusting

¼ tsp salt

100g unsalted butter, diced,
  plus extra for greasing

1 medium egg, lightly beaten

FILLING

6 medium eggs, beaten

300g freshly cooked Beneforté
  broccoli

150g Norfolk Dapple cheese
  or Gruyère, coarsely grated

Small bunch fresh chives, chopped

225ml double cream

Good pinch mustard powder

Salt and freshly ground pepper

*Serve with a dressed rocket salad.
For a lighter version, try using
low-fat yoghurt with a little milk
instead of cream.*

Preheat the oven to 200°C/fan 180°C/gas 6. Put a baking tray in the oven to warm through ready to cook the pastry case on. Butter and dust a 23cm wide, 4cm deep, fluted, loose-bottomed flan tin.

Put the flour, salt and butter in a food processor and whizz to fine breadcrumbs. Then, with the machine still running, add the egg and continue to whizz until the pastry starts to stick together (add a teaspoon or two of water if it's too dry). Bring together into a ball and knead briefly until smooth. Roll out on a lightly floured surface, use to line the prepared tart tin and trim the edges. Chill for 20 minutes.

Prick the pastry base with a fork and line with baking parchment and baking beans. Place on the preheated baking tray and bake for 10 minutes. Remove the paper and beans and bake for a further 10 minutes. Brush the pastry with a little of the beaten eggs (for the filling) and bake for a further 5 minutes, until pale golden. Remove from the oven and reduce the temperature to 180°C/fan 160°C/gas 4.

Meanwhile, bring a pan of water to the boil. Add the broccoli and cook for 2–3 minutes. Drain well, refresh in cold water, then drain again.

Sprinkle the cheese, broccoli and chives evenly over the base of the pastry case. Beat the eggs with the cream, add the mustard powder and season well, then pour into the pastry case. Bake for 25–30 minutes until the filling is just set and pale golden in places. Cool in the tin for 5 minutes, then remove and serve warm or at room temperature.

Indulgent tomato and fig tart

'Cornerways is Britain's largest single-structure glasshouse, covering 18 hectares and producing 140 million tonnes of tomatoes annually. We supply a wide variety of tomatoes to the largest UK supermarkets as well as to smaller local customers, such as farm shops, restaurants, village stores and florists. We have 20,000 British native bumblebees living in 400 beehives pollinating the tomato plants, and annually 115 million litres of rainwater is collected from the glasshouse roof, which is used for irrigation. The nursery is next to the British Sugar Factory, and we are able to use recycled heat and carbon dioxide for energy-efficient tomato growing.'

Cornerways

serves 6-8

1 tbsp dried mixed herbs

250g ready-made all-butter
   puff pastry

225g British vine-ripened
   cocktail tomatoes

5 fresh figs

140g British cherry tomatoes

120g sun-dried tomato pesto

140g soft goat's cheese, crumbled,
   such as Ellingham

2 tbsp thyme sprigs

2 tbsp runny honey

Preheat the oven to 220°C/fan 200°C/gas 7. Oil a 30cm pizza tin.

Sprinkle the herbs over the pastry and then roll out to a thickness of 5mm. Use to fill the pizza tin, then prick all over with a fork. Chill for about 20 minutes.

Quarter the cocktail tomatoes and figs and halve the cherry tomatoes. Spread a little sun-dried tomato pesto over the pastry. Arrange the tomatoes and figs on the top. Top with the crumbled goat's cheese, followed by the thyme. Drizzle with a little honey.

Bake for 14 minutes. Cool on a wire rack for 5 minutes before serving.

This is an ideal recipe to serve for high tea with a crisp salad. You could also make 12 individual tarts instead. In this case, cut the pastry into 9cm rounds and bake for 10–12 minutes.

Aunty Rosie's creamy onion tart

'Aunty Rosie's big house in London is where the family congregates when there is something to celebrate: a birthday, a christening, an anniversary, Christmas or just a Saturday teatime when a few of us are in the neighbourhood. She has an astonishing way of magicking up a buffet to suit all tastes, and in pride of place there is always a creamy onion tart.'

Dame Stella Rimington DCB, author and former Director General of MI5

This recipe is sponsored by RG Abrey Farms, whose fresh produce site is located in the heart of the Breckland. Started in 1939 by the late Russell Gordon Abrey, it is now a third-generation family farming business.

serves 6–8

675g large onions (not reds)

1 tsp sugar

75g butter

3 tbsp olive oil

40g flour

3 large eggs

3 large egg yolks

450ml single cream
    or milk and cream (the addition
    of milk gives a lighter texture)

1 tbsp snipped fresh chives,
    plus extra to serve

100g Norfolk Dapple cheese
    or similar hard cheese, grated

Freshly grated nutmeg

Salt and freshly ground pepper

250g ready-made shortcrust pastry

Preheat the oven to 190°C/fan 170°C/gas 5. Butter a 24cm wide, 4cm deep loose-bottomed flan tin.

Slice the onions thickly and sprinkle them with the sugar. Heat the butter and oil in a frying pan on a low heat and cook the onions for a good 30 minutes, stirring occasionally, until golden brown. Stir in the flour and cook for a further 2 minutes to cook the flour. Set aside to cool.

In a large bowl, beat together the eggs and yolks, the cream, chives and cheese, then pour into the onion mix, stirring gently together. Season to taste with nutmeg, salt and pepper. It is the nutmeg that adds such a distinctive and delicate flavour to this flan but the precise quantity is a matter of taste.

Roll the pastry out and use to line the prepared flan tin. Trim the edges. Fill with the mixture and cook for 25–30 minutes until just set and golden. Serve with freshly chopped chives on top.

Toss a little crumbled blue cheese on the top to give another dimension to this lovely tart.

Cromer crab, rocket & ricotta tart

'The Britons Arms has been trading since 1951 and has become something of an institution. We are fortunate in occupying one of the most attractive properties in Norwich: everyone's idea of a medieval thatched building. It has recently been renovated by the Norwich Preservation Trust with grants from English Heritage. With a new thatch and a state-of-the-art kitchen, we are at our very best. We have been using this enriched yeast-based dough for our tart bases for years. It comes from the wonderful Greens Cookbook, a storehouse of exciting vegetarian recipes from the restaurant of the same name overlooking San Francisco Bay.'

Sue Skipper and Gilly Mixer, The Britons Arms, Norwich

serves 8–10

DOUGH
350g plain flour
7g (1 sachet) dried yeast
175g butter, soft
Pinch salt
150ml warm water
2 eggs

FILLING
3 dressed Cromer crabs
   or 300g mixed crabmeat
50g peppery rocket leaves
250g tub good quality ricotta
   cheese
250ml double cream
4 eggs
Pinch salt

Begin the dough at least an hour before you want to start cooking.

Quickly and lightly blitz the flour, dried yeast, butter and salt in the food processor using the pulse function until the mixture resembles fine breadcrumbs. Transfer to a good-sized mixing bowl and make a well in the centre. Into this, pour the warm water and eggs. Incorporate these with a flexible spatula until you have a wet, smooth dough. Try not to handle it.

Place a cloth over the bowl and leave it to rise in a warm place for about an hour. It should double in size and have a bubbling, slightly fermenting look about it.

Preheat the oven to 220°C/fan 200°C/gas 7 and put in a baking sheet to heat up. Oil and gently warm a 30cm ceramic flan dish.

Turn the dough into the flan dish, pushing it firmly but gently to the sides. It should be rather thicker at the sides than on the bottom. Don't expect it to 'stay put' – it's not pastry. Set aside in a cool place.

To make the filling, take the crabmeat from the shells and lightly mix the white and dark meat together. Distribute over the dough base. Using a pair of kitchen scissors, roughly 'chop' the rocket over the crab and then spoon over the ricotta in smallish dollops. Measure the cream in a jug, add the eggs and salt, lightly whisk and pour over the other ingredients.

Place in the middle shelf of the oven on a baking sheet and bake for about 1 hour until the centre is firm. If after 30 minutes the tart shows any sign of burning, turn the oven down to 200°C/180°fan/gas 6.

Cromer lobster & crab tartines

'Robbie and I opened the Rocket House Café in Cromer in 2006. Our wonderful location overlooking the beach means that we can watch our most prized produce arriving on fishing boats nearly every morning from March to November. Cromer crab and lobster feature regularly on our menus and are enjoyed by both staff and customers. We also pickle and preserve vegetables grown on our allotment by the green-fingered Jane, which keep us going throughout the winter months. This dish typifies everything we love about cooking in Cromer.'

Robbie and Genevieve Bloomfield, Rocket House Café, Cromer

makes 12 bite-size

FILLING

24 small tips Norfolk samphire

½ tsp fennel seeds, toasted
    in a dry pan (be careful not to burn)

¼ tsp dried chilli flakes

Pinch sea salt

1 medium dressed Cromer crab
    or 100g mixed crabmeat

½ tsp lemon zest

CANAPÉ CASES

4–6 slices medium sliced processed
    white bread, crusts removed

25ml extra virgin rapeseed oil

TO ASSEMBLE

½ dressed Cromer lobster

Pickled cucumber, sliced with
    a vegetable peeler into 12 strips

½ lemon

Cook the samphire in boiling water for 3–4 minutes, drain and then plunge into iced water. When cool, drain and set aside for later.

Grind the fennel seeds, chilli flakes and sea salt in a pestle and mortar. Combine with the crabmeat and the lemon zest. Refrigerate until needed.

For the cases, preheat the oven to 200°C/fan 180°C/gas 6. Use a 12-hole mini muffin tray or 12 fluted mini moulds. Roll each slice of bread out very thinly. Cut out rounds, brush with a little oil and fit into the moulds, pressing down. Bake for about 5 minutes until pale and golden. Cool on a wire rack.

To assemble the canapés, cut the lobster into 12 thin, even slices. Any leftover lobster meat can be diced finely and added to your crab mix. Pat dry the cucumber slices with kitchen paper and curl a piece in the base of each case, then top with teaspoonful of the crab. Arrange 2 sprigs of the Norfolk samphire on top of the crab and top each tartine with a slice of lobster.

Squeeze over a little lemon juice just before serving.

Only squeeze over the lemon juice immediately before serving or the sweetness of the crab might be lost.

Cromer crab rarebit

The style of The Pigs is proudly British and very local. You will see dishes from the past back in vogue at The Pigs, and cuts of meat forgotten in recent years used to great effect. This recipe uses a unique local product: world-famous Cromer crab, a fresh brown crab prized for its high proportion of white meat to dark, and its tender, sweet qualities attributed to the fact they grow slowly on the chalk reef just off the coast. Male edible crabs are referred to as cocks and females as hens. Cocks have more sweet white meat; hens have more rich brown meat.

The Pigs, Edgefield

serves 6

20g butter

20g plain flour

120ml milk

2 eggs, separated

2 tbsp Worcestershire sauce

1 tbsp Tabasco sauce

1 tbsp Colman's mustard powder

60g Norfolk Dapple or a similar
   hard Cheddar-type cheese, grated

250g Cromer crab meat
   (white and brown)

Salt and freshly ground pepper

2 tbsp finely chopped flat-leaf parsley

Half a lemon

6 slices sourdough bread

Melt the butter in a medium saucepan, then add the flour and stir to form a roux. Cook over a gentle heat, stirring with a wooden spoon, making sure you cook the flour through. This will take a couple of minutes – it is important to cook well as this gives a wonderful nutty flavour to the rarebit.

Slowly pour the milk into the pan, whisking thoroughly, until smooth and creamy and the sauce is thoroughly cooked, then set aside to cool slightly.

Stir the egg yolks into the cooled roux, along with the Worcestershire and Tabasco sauces, mustard powder and grated cheese, until well combined.

Now add the cooked crabmeat, season lightly to taste, then mix in the parsley and a squeeze of lemon juice.

In a clean bowl whisk the egg whites until stiff then fold into the mixture.

Toast the bread lightly, place on a wire rack and spread generously with the crab mix. Cook under a medium grill until slightly puffed up, golden brown and bubbling. Serve immediately.

Spicy Cromer crab cakes

Gurneys was set up by Mike Gurney around forty years ago when he learned to grow oysters in the creeks and to smoke fish. The first fish shop in Brancaster was just ten square feet and known as the Hole in the Wall. In 1992 the Burnham Market shop opened, selling the very best in locally produced smoked fish, shellfish and wet fish, mainly landed locally. Today Gurneys is a thriving fishmongers' managed by good friends Matt Falvey, Ned Catt and Alastair Steele. All three are 'hooked' on knowing all there is to know about cooking and preparing fish.

Gurneys Fish Shop

makes 10

Oil, to fry the crab cakes

CRAB CAKES

4 dressed Cromer crabs
    or 400g mixed crabmeat

100g fresh white breadcrumbs

2 spring onions, finely chopped

Half red chilli (seeds optional),
    finely chopped

1 kaffir lime leaf, very finely chopped

2 tbsp finely chopped coriander

1 tbsp finely grated ginger

1 tbsp lime juice

1 large egg, beaten

1 tsp salt

1 tsp white pepper

SAFFRON MAYONNAISE

2 large egg yolks

½ tsp Dijon mustard

1 tsp cider vinegar

1 garlic clove, crushed

Salt and freshly ground pepper,
    to taste

175ml sunflower oil

75ml extra virgin olive oil

Pinch saffron infused in 1 tbsp water

Combine all the ingredients for the crab cakes in a bowl and mix well. Divide the mixture into 10 equal pieces and roll to form balls, then gently flatten with the palm of your hand, but not too thin. If you want to check the seasoning or heat at this point, fry a small amount, taste and add more salt, pepper or chilli if required. Then chill the crab cakes to allow the mixture to set.

In either a bowl or a food processor, put the egg yolks, mustard, vinegar, garlic, salt and pepper and whisk. Combine the two oils then slowly drizzle in a little at a time, keeping the processor running continuously, or whisking continuously if making by hand. When half the oil has been added, stir in the infused saffron then continue to pour in the rest of the oil until thick and creamy. Taste and season if needed.

Fry the crab cakes until lightly browned on both sides, then serve with the saffron mayonnaise.

Lovely for high tea or, made smaller, as delicious hot canapés.

Curried Cromer crab mayonnaise on tomatoes

'On my second Sunday as Bishop of Norwich, in February 2000, I went to Cromer. I was launched into the sea on the lifeboat before leading a service in the parish church. Within a week or two I was back to watch Cromer crabs being dressed. It felt like I was tasting crab for the first time. There are lots of reasons to love living in Norfolk and its food is one of them.'

The Bishop of Norwich

This recipe is sponsored by G.R. Bunning & Co, known locally as 'Bunning's Fish', legendary fishmongers based in the old village blacksmith's at Cranworth in the heart of Norfolk.

serves 6

3 or 4 medium vine tomatoes

5 tbsp good quality mayonnaise

Pinch each ground turmeric, coriander, cumin, ginger, chilli

½ tsp lemon juice

2 dashes Tabasco sauce

500g fresh white Cromer crab meat

Salt and freshly ground pepper

6 slices sourdough or ciabatta

50g washed and dried lamb's lettuce, roots trimmed

2 tsp extra virgin olive oil

Thinly slice the tomatoes.

In a bowl measure out the mayonnaise and stir in the spices, then add the lemon juice and Tabasco sauce. Fold the crab into the mixture and season to taste.

Lightly toast the slices of bread.

Place 3 or 4 slices of tomato on each piece of toasted bread and spoon on the crab mayonnaise. Toss the lamb's lettuce in olive oil and garnish the toast with it.

Potted Norfolk shrimps with chives

'Stangroom Bros is a family farming business established in 1870. We began growing mint for Colman's of Norwich in 1967, with 3 hectares. Since then our herb hectareage has increased to 125. We now grow, dry and process parsley, tarragon, chives, oregano, sage and coriander as well as mint. Our commitment is to ensuring our crops are safe, wholesome and meet agreed quality standards. Experiment with all the herbs in your garden – you will be surprised what a difference herbs make.'

Di Stangroom, Stangroom Bros Ltd

makes 4

200g butter
Good pinch ground mace
Good pinch freshly grated nutmeg
Good pinch cayenne pepper
Freshly ground black pepper
1 tbsp finely chopped fresh chives
Zest ½ lemon, finely chopped
250g brown shrimps or prawns, cooked and peeled

Put 100g of the butter into a saucepan and allow it to melt over a low heat. Remove the pan from the heat and leave the melted butter to cool, but not set. This will allow the milk solids to sink to the bottom of the pan so you can spoon off the clear, clarified butter later.

Place the rest of the butter, the spices, cayenne and a good amount of black pepper in a saucepan and melt slowly over a low heat. When it has melted, remove the pan from the heat and add the chives, lemon zest and shrimps, stirring well.

Divide the shrimp mixture between four 125ml jars or ramekins. Take the pan with the melted butter and spoon the clarified butter over the shrimp mixture, tilting the pan slightly will help you get the clarified butter more easily.

Cover the jars with cling film and chill for a good 1½ hours.

Remove the potted shrimps from the fridge 30 minutes before serving and serve with warm crusty bread.

The cayenne gives this a lovely piquancy. Feel free to add more or less depending on how much warmth you like.

Vegetable salad with nuts & squash ketchup

Titchwell Manor is a stunning boutique hotel a stone's throw from the North Norfolk coast, offering award-winning dining and celebrated gastronomy in the informal eating rooms complete with sea-view terrace or in the fine-dining conservatory. Rising culinary star Eric Snaith is behind the stoves with his talented brigade. His flair and flavours have earned him a reputation for innovative, modern European food using the finest local ingredients. The hotel is also famous for its afternoon teas.

Titchwell Manor

serves 6

DRESSING

Half a lemon

Half an orange

1 tsp chardonnay vinegar

4 tbsp extra virgin rapeseed oil

Maldon salt, to taste

1 tsp honey

SQUASH KETCHUP

1 small shallot, sliced

80g butter

200g diced butternut squash

50g white wine vinegar

50g sugar

1 clove

6 coriander seeds

Salt

SALAD

6 new potatoes

3 tbsp chopped parsley, oregano
and dill

1 tbsp toasted mixed seeds,
such as fennel, coriander, pumpkin
and sunflower

2 tbsp roasted and chopped nuts,
such as hazelnut, almond and
pine nut

80g Fielding Cottage goat's cheese,
thinly sliced

2 tbsp each thinly sliced purple
and Romanesque cauliflower

2 tbsp diced cooked beetroot

Roast the orange and lemon on a baking tray at 180°C/160°C/gas 4 until they start to burn round the edges. Squeeze the juice into a mixing bowl and whisk together with all the other dressing ingredients. Add the orange and lemon halves and allow to infuse overnight.

For the ketchup, cook the shallot in the butter in a pan on a medium heat. When soft, add the remaining ingredients, including salt to taste and enough water to cover. Cook until nearly all the water has gone and the squash is very soft. Purée, taste and adjust the seasoning; adjust the acidity with a little more vinegar if necessary.

For the salad, boil the potatoes until just cooked, allow to cool and then smoke in a smoker or on a barbecue. Chill and slice. Toss all the ingredients together in a large bowl with the dressing. Serve with the squash ketchup in a dish on the side, or divide into portions and serve the salad on top of the squash ketchup.

Mrs Temple's Binham Blue, pear, sage and walnut frittata

Stephen and Catherine keep Brown Swiss cattle at Wighton near Wells-next-the Sea. They began to make cheese in 2000 and produce both hard and soft varieties. The dairy is carbon neutral, even carbon negative, as the whey that runs from the curds as they metamorphose into cheese and the cow manure are transformed through anaerobic digestion to create heat, electricity and a fibrous composted fertiliser that conditions the soil, ready to grow further nutritious crops for the cows to eat. Full circle. 'This frittata is inspired by a recipe published by Margaret's Tea Rooms of Baconsthorpe.'

Stephen and Catherine Temple, Mrs Temple's Cheese

serves 6

100g onion, finely chopped

1 tbsp rapeseed oil

3 pears, quartered, cored and each quarter sliced into 3

100g Binham Blue cheese, cubed

1 tbsp fresh sage, chopped

100g walnut pieces

8 medium eggs

Sea salt and freshly ground pepper

Preheat the oven to 180°C/fan 160°C/gas 4. Line a 6-hole muffin mould or tin with tulip cases.

In a small pan, fry the onion in the rapeseed oil until lightly golden. Arrange the sliced pears in the muffin cases so they stand up. Divide the Binham cheese cubes between the cases, then add the cooked onion, chopped sage and walnut pieces. Whisk the eggs in a bowl until the yolks are well mixed into the whites. Season well and pour over the pear, onion, cheese and nut mixture.

Bake in the oven for 25–35 minutes until set and golden. Allow to cool for 10 minutes before serving with a seasonal salad.

Norfolk County asparagus torte

Norfolk County English asparagus is grown on the light sandy soils of Breckland. Asparagus is quite a tradition in Breckland. There are photos from 1930s showing teams of women harvesting and packing the tender spears. Tim Jolly and his family have farmed at Roudham, Norfolk for over twenty-five years, producing premium quality asparagus. 'Our customers range from London restaurants and catering companies to specialist grocers, and all of them want to offer the best quality English asparagus. Every year letters and tweets arrive from appreciative Norfolk County asparagus lovers.' Tim and his family host occasional open days.

Tim and Ellen Jolly, Norfolk County Asparagus

serves 6–8

40g butter

150g Mrs Temple's Norfolk Alpine cheese or Parmesan, finely grated

2 bunches local asparagus, washed, woody ends snapped off

2 banana shallots or 1 medium onion, finely chopped

A little light oil

2 large eggs plus 1 egg yolk

225ml double cream

Salt and freshly ground pepper

2 tbsp finely chopped parsley

Preheat the oven to 200°C/fan 180°/gas 6. Prepare a 20cm springform tin: line the base and lower edge with baking parchment then, using a little of the butter, grease the base and sides, and finally dust well with some of the grated cheese.

Cut the tips off the asparagus, reserve them, then very finely chop the rest of the spears.

In a heavy-based pan, soften the finely chopped shallots in the butter with a dash of oil. Then add the finely chopped asparagus and cook slowly until just soft but still bright green. Remove from the pan and set aside, then gently cook the tips until just softening and set those aside too.

Whisk the eggs and cream together until smooth. Season with salt and pepper, then stir in the parsley, the remaining grated cheese and the chopped asparagus and shallots.

Pour into the prepared tin and scatter with the softened tips. Stand on a baking tray and cook for 30–35 minutes. It needs to be just set and golden – try not to overcook it.

You could describe this as a crust-less quiche, but it's much more than that: gluten-free, rich, creamy and full of asparagus, with a cheesy edge. Lovely with tossed salad leaves and crusty bread or new season potatoes.

Hoisin duck lettuce parcels

'We breed, hatch, rear, then prepare Gressingham Duck on Red Tractor-assured farms in Norfolk and Suffolk. The Gressingham duck is a breed that first came about when the small but flavourful wild Mallard was crossed with the larger Pekin duck, giving a meaty, succulent duck with more breast meat, less fat and a rich gamey flavour. We believe that delicious duck comes from responsible farming and that cooking with duck makes a meal far more memorable. Duck tastes wonderful, is one of the healthier meats and is far easier to cook than people think.'

Vernon Blackmore, development chef at Gressingham Duck

serves 5

4 Gressingham duck legs

Salt and freshly ground pepper

1 lime, zest and juice

2 spring onions,
    finely chopped into rings

3 tbsp hoisin sauce

Small bunch coriander, leaves
roughly chopped

12 mint leaves, middle stem
    removed, finely chopped

10 Little Gem lettuce leaves

Preheat the oven to 190°C/fan 170°C/gas 5.

Prick the skin of the duck legs with a skewer or fork and season. Place on a baking tray and cook for about 1 hour 15 minutes. Remove from the oven, pour off the excess fat and allow them to cool.

While the duck legs are cooling, mix together the lime, onions, hoisin sauce, coriander and mint.

Once the legs are cool enough to handle, remove the skin and cut into thin strips; set aside. Pull the duck meat from the bone, roughly dice and place in a mixing bowl. Be careful to look out for any small bones as you do this.

Add the lime and spring onion mixture to the duck. Mix well, check for seasoning, adjust as necessary, then spoon a small amount into each lettuce leaf, scatter over the crispy skin and serve.

Have all the ingredients prepared ahead and assemble them just before serving them so the Little Gem leaves stay fresh and crisp.

Potted Norfolk quail

'Cooking is a passion for me. I really enjoy cooking for friends and family, especially using our own ethically farmed quail. Potted quail is a delight to make and stores well. It is a lovely savoury addition to high tea, but could equally be used as a canapé or starter at a dinner party, served with crackers or fresh, crusty bread. This recipe also works well with other game birds, such as pheasant or partridge, if you have a glut after a successful shoot.'

Ellie Savory, farmer's wife and director of Norfolk Quail

serves 2–4

2 Norfolk quail

1 litre vegetable stock (see below)

50g butter, soft

2 tbsp chopped chives

Salt and freshly ground pepper

VEGETABLE STOCK

1.5 litres water

3 carrots

2 celery sticks

1 onion

1 bay leaf

3 thyme sprigs

6 cloves

1 allspice berry

6 juniper berries

Put all the vegetable stock ingredients into a large saucepan, bring to the boil and simmer for a good half hour, then strain and return the clear stock to the pan.

Add the quail to the vegetable stock and poach very gently at no more than 60°C for approximately 4 hours.

Allow the pan to cool slightly, remove the quail from the poaching liquid and strip the meat from the birds.

Mix the quail meat together with the butter in a bowl, fold in the chopped chives, taste and add the seasoning. Place the mixture in a serving dish.

Serve at room temperature with fresh bread rolls, slices of sourdough or toast, and a good apple or pear chutney.

This will keep in the fridge for 4–6 weeks if potted into sterilised jars, sealed and submerged in 90°C-plus water for 20 minutes.

Baked chicken & ham pancake

'The Imperial Hotel is family owned and managed and has just celebrated trading as the same family business for 80 years. Our Baked Chicken and Ham Pancake has been a firm favourite since our restaurant opened in 1972. It was introduced to the Imperial Hotel by Roger Mobbs in the Rambouillet Restaurant. We have changed the restaurant a bit since then and renamed it Café Cru. We have also opened the Terrace with stunning sea views, but it seems there can be no change where this dish is concerned. If we try to take it off the menu, there is a customer protest.'

The Imperial Hotel, Great Yarmouth

serves 6

VELOUTÉ FILLING
450g cooked chicken breasts
450g cooked smoked ham joint
55g butter
55g flour
568ml chicken stock, hot
Salt and freshly ground pepper

PANCAKES
3 medium eggs
175g plain flour
425ml milk
2 tbsp vegetable oil,
    plus extra for cooking

TO FINISH
568ml double cream
225g cheese, such as Mrs Temple's
    Alpine or Cheddar, grated
1 tbsp chopped parsley

Cut the cooked chicken and ham into 1cm square cubes, making sure all the fat is removed.

Make the chicken velouté by melting the butter slowly in a thick-bottomed pan. Once melted, add the flour to make a roux, and cook for a few minutes to thoroughly cook out the raw flour taste. Slowly add the hot chicken stock and whisk to ensure there are no lumps. Season with salt and pepper, bring to the boil, add the diced chicken and ham then remove from the heat.

To make the pancakes, crack the eggs into the flour in a bowl and slowly add the milk to make a batter, ensuring there are no lumps. Mix in the vegetable oil – this helps the mixture not to stick when cooking.

Pour 100ml batter mix into a lightly oiled, hot, shallow pan, colour one side, then flip over. Remove from the pan to cool on a plate. Repeat the process until you have 6 pancakes.

Meanwhile, preheat the oven to 180°C/fan 160°C/gas 4.

When all the pancakes are cooked, spoon about 175g filling into the centre of each one and tuck the sides in to form parcels. Place in individual dishes topped with double cream and grated cheese. Bake for 10 minutes. Sprinkle with parsley and serve.

A veggie alternative could be wild mushrooms with cranberries, topped with cream and soft goat's cheese.

Venison & chicken liver parfait

'I grew up on the family arable farm in Dilham, which my great-grandfather moved to in 1936. I started cooking at an early age; I can remember baking with my granny Elsie. I am mostly self-taught. My other passion in life is hunting. I was introduced to deerstalking in 2012. After applying for a deer rifle I shot my first red deer on Christmas Eve. I butcher my own game as well. This recipe is quite versatile. If you find it difficult to find venison, pork liver is a good alternative. Cook the parfait in anything you like; I make lots of different sizes.

Guy Paterson, Country Landowners' Association Game Chef of the Year 2014

makes 1.5kg

REDUCTION

120g shallots

3 garlic cloves

4 thyme sprigs

30g butter

250ml port

PARFAIT

300g venison liver

400g chicken liver

6 medium eggs

25g salt

30 grinds pepper

5g caster sugar

450g butter

Preheat the oven to 120°C/fan 100°C/gas 1.

Allow the ingredients to reach room temperature. Slice the shallots and garlic, pick the thyme from the sprigs. Melt the butter in a medium saucepan and sweat down the shallots, garlic and thyme until soft. Add the port to the pan and simmer until almost all the liquid has evaporated.

Put the reduction in a large food processor or blender along with all the other ingredients apart from the butter. Melt the butter separately. Blend the liver mix until it is a thick, liquid consistency. Add the butter and blend again.

Here's the tricky part: pour some of the parfait into a metal sieve over a large bowl and, using a ladle, push the mix through the sieve. Between each batch I rinse the sieve. Now pour the parfait mix into a 1.5-litre terrine dish and cover with cling film.

Boil the kettle and put enough water in a large roasting tray to make a bain-marie. Place the parfait dish in the bain-marie and bake it in the oven for approximately 30 minutes. To check if the parfait is cooked, gently nudge the dish. If it does not move, it's done.

Once cooked, remove from oven and the bain-marie and allow to cool before refrigerating.

Make the parfait in 12 x 150ml pots as great little Christmas gifts; cook for 14 minutes. Crab-apple jelly is a very good accompaniment, cutting through the richness of the parfait.

Sausage, chicken & apple pie

Arthur Howell is a fourth-generation butcher and a familiar face in North Norfolk food and drink circles. Arthur's great-grandfather founded their family business in 1889 and it continues to supply first-class meat from its three shops in Binham, Burnham Market and Wells-next-the-Sea. Known for his trademark red coat and cheery smile, Arthur received the Individual Food Hero Award at Aylsham Show, and was named East Anglian Champion in the Farm Shop & Deli Awards in 2014.

Arthur Howell

serves 10

PASTRY

450g plain white flour

Pinch salt

300g butter

1 egg

A little cold water

FILLING

500g good quality butcher's
    sausagemeat

50g fresh breadcrumbs

1 tbsp freshly chopped parsley

200g smoked bacon, chopped

1 lemon, zest and juice

2 large eggs

Salt and freshly ground pepper

500g boneless, skinless
    chicken breasts

175g button mushrooms,
    finely sliced

140g dessert apple, sliced,
    or dried apple slices

1 egg, beaten, to glaze

Alpine or Cheddar, grated

1 tbsp chopped parsley

This pie freezes brilliantly uncooked. If you are in a hurry, use a good ready-made all-butter shortcrust pastry.

Butter a 25cm-wide, 7cm-deep springform tin and line the base with baking parchment.

Place the flour and salt in a food processor, add the butter and blitz until it resembles fine crumbs. Incorporate the egg and blitz again. While the motor is running, add a little water to bring the dough together in lumps. Transfer to a bowl and finish by hand. Wrap in cling film and rest in the fridge for at least an hour.

Preheat the oven to 190°C/fan 170°C/gas 5.

Roll out three-quarters of the pastry and line the springform tin, easing out folds and pressing well into the sides. Stand the tin in the fridge, with the remaining pastry wrapped so it doesn't dry out.

In a large bowl put the sausagemeat, breadcrumbs, parsley, bacon, lemon zest and juice and eggs. Mix well and season with a little salt and some pepper.

With a sharp knife, butterfly the chicken breasts: slice horizontally from one side to the other, being careful not to cut right through, then open them out like a butterfly. Press between cling film or in a freezer bag using a rolling pin until of an equal thickness.

To layer up the pie, first spread half of the sausagemeat mixture over the base of the lined tin, then follow with half the mushrooms, then the apple slices. Lay the chicken breasts on top, followed by, again in layers, the rest of the apple, the mushroom and the sausagemeat.

Roll out a pastry lid, cut and place on top of the pie, pressing the edges together. Crimp between your fingers to seal. Decorate with any leftover pastry. If you are going to freeze the pie, do so at this stage.

Make a hole in the centre, brush with beaten egg to glaze and bake for 1½ hours. Cool, then chill before serving.

Pork & pigeon pie

Sarah has long been an advocate for Norfolk and its food. She set up her business in beautiful converted flint barns overlooking the coast at Cley and Blakeney. She and the Bray's Cottage team make her famous pork pies which can be found in all the best Norfolk establishments and, increasingly, nationally. She adds a cook's flair to her pies, using seasonal ingredients such as local wild garlic, apple from Sandringham and even fig and orange. News reached pie fan Heston Blumenthal, who invited her to appear on one of his programmes, where they swapped techniques during breaks in filming.

Sarah Pettegree, Bray's Cottage Pork Pies

serves 6 – 8

HOT WATER CRUST PASTRY
260g lard melted, warm
360g strong white flour
350g plain flour
375ml hot water
2 tsp salt
2 tsp sugar

PORK AND PIGEON MIX
70g dry-cured smoked bacon lardons
150g traditional sausagemeat
500g pork shoulder meat, cut into 1cm dice
¼ tsp nutmeg
1 tsp paprika
1 bay leaf, rolled and finely chopped
2 tsp salt
1 tsp ground pepper
4 pigeon breasts

In the winter months you could use partridge or pheasant with the pork. Add extra flavour using fresh herbs or even fruit, such as apricots or redcurrants.

Line a 15cm-deep springform tin with baking parchment if it's not non-stick.

Mix all the pastry ingredients together, kneading well until it has a firm consistency and all the flour is combined. Leave to cool to room temperature, covered with cling film or in a plastic bag.

For the filling, mix the bacon lardons, sausagemeat and pork, and season with the spices, salt and pepper. If you want to test the seasoning, fry a dessertspoon of mix until cooked through to taste.

Preheat the oven to 180°C/160°C fan/gas 4.

Once the pastry is cool, lightly flour the work surface and roll out the dough to 1cm thick, large enough to line the tin, with a 2cm excess above the sides. Save the trimmings to make the lid. Lift the pastry into the tin and line it, using your fingers to smooth out the sides. Roll out the remaining pastry and cut around the tin, making the lid slightly bigger than the tin.

Take half the meat mixture and fill the base of the tin. Top with a layer of pigeon breasts, followed by the rest of the pork mix. Fill to just below the top of the tin. Brush the edges with cold water using a pastry brush and cover with the pastry lid. Then, using your thumb and forefinger, crimp the edge to seal. Make a hole in the centre of the lid for the steam to escape. Decorate with any remaining pastry.

Cook on a baking sheet for a good 2½ hours until the centre of the pie reaches at least 75°C and all the visible pastry is well cooked. Leave to cool completely so the juices set before cutting.

Sausage rolls with roasted vegetables

'My great-grandfather, Dr Andrew Kaye, kept indigenous Large Black pigs in his orchard at Blakeney between the wars, sending the meat to London along with apples from the orchard to top up his income as a rural GP. At Scott's Field Pork we are doing things the new old-fashioned way. From the now rare Large Black we produce meat that appeals to modern tastes while retaining the succulence and flavour of an old breed. We are part of a Field to Fork food web whereby local butchers, Impsons of Swaffham, supply our pork to Strattons, where it is used with Elveden vegetables and flour from Heygates to produce this special sausage roll.'

Rob Simonds, Scott's Field Pork

makes 10

450g butternut squash, peeled
    and chopped into 5mm dice
225g shallots, finely sliced
1 tsp smoked paprika
2 tsp caraway seeds
1 tbsp rapeseed oil
Salt and freshly ground pepper
225g carrots, grated
4 garlic cloves, finely chopped
2 tbsp sage, chopped
900g rare-breed or good quality
    pork sausagemeat
250g all-butter puff pastry
1 egg, beaten
1 tsp sesame seeds
1 tsp poppy seeds

Replace sausagemeat with nut roast for a vegetarian version.

Preheat the oven to 180°C/fan 160°C/gas 4.

Place the butternut squash and sliced shallots in a deep roasting pan with the paprika, caraway and oil. Season well and roast, uncovered, for 20 minutes, turning with a slice halfway through cooking. Remove from the oven and allow to cool while preparing the meat mix.

Turn the oven up to 20°C/fan 180°C/gas 6.

In a large bowl mix the carrots, garlic and sage with the sausagemeat. Add the roasted butternut squash and shallots and mix well with your hands until the ingredients are well combined.

Roll out the pastry to a long rectangle approximately 80x20cm. Shape the sausagemeat mix into an 80cm long sausage. Place the sausage in the middle of the pastry and egg wash the long sides. Wrap one side of the pastry around the sausage and press it in place with your hands; fold the other side over and seal. Turn the sausage over and shape with your hands to make it even.

Cut into 10 sausage rolls. Make several slashes with a knife across each roll to allow steam to escape while cooking and for the pastry to cook crisply. Brush with the egg wash and sprinkle with the sesame and poppy seeds. Place on a large baking sheet. Bake the sausage rolls in the hot oven for 30 minutes until crisp and golden. Best eaten when still warm.

Spanish teatime savouries

'The combination of chorizo, eggs and red pepper is classically Spanish and something you might expect to find on your plate for desayuno, that second savoury breakfast taken mid-morning to tide you over until lunchtime, but I think it makes an ideal tea-time savoury nibble. You don't want to be bothering with knives and forks at tea-time – it's a finger food type of meal, so I have used quail's eggs to keep these savouries bite-sized and delicate.'

Roger Hickman, Chef/proprietor, Roger Hickman's Restaurant, Norwich

makes 12 bite-size

4 slices soft white spelt bread

Olive oil

250g baby spinach

25g butter

Pinch salt

2 cooking chorizos

12 quail's eggs

Smoked paprika (dulce/sweet)

RED PEPPER PUREE

3 red Romano peppers, sliced

1 red chilli, seeds removed, chopped

3 garlic cloves, finely chopped

2 shallots, finely chopped

First make the red pepper purée. Preheat the oven to 180°C/160°C/gas 4. Put the peppers, chilli, garlic and shallots in a roasting tray and roast in the oven for 15 minutes. Blitz in a food processor and pass the purée through a fine sieve. Set aside.

To make the croutons, cut out 12 discs of bread using a 3cm ring. Fry the bread discs slowly in a little olive oil until just coloured. Don't let the oil get too hot as the bread will brown. When one side is cooked, turn and repeat. Drain the croutons on kitchen paper.

Pick the stalks off the spinach and wilt the leaves in a pan with the butter and salt. Remove as soon as all the spinach has gone limp – this shouldn't take more than a minute. Cool the spinach on kitchen paper to absorb the excess moisture.

Skin the chorizos and cut into twelve 7–8mm slices. Gently fry them in a little olive oil for about 90 seconds on each side to firm up rather than colour them.

Oil a 3cm ring and put it in a small frying pan with some olive oil. Break a quail's egg into it and fry on a low heat for 30 seconds. If the top is not cooked enough, finish under the grill – don't overcook the bottom. Easiest is to do this in a batch of 4, repeated 3 times.

To assemble the savouries, put some spinach on each of the croutons. Place a slice of chorizo on each, spread some red pepper purée on the chorizo (this will help the egg stay put, as well as adding a delicious Spanish flavour twist), top with an egg, and sprinkle with sweet smoked paprika.

Black pudding & pancetta Scotch eggs

'The Fruit Pig Company is East Anglia's only traditional breeds butchery supported by the Rare Breed Survival Trust and the British Pig Association. It delivers to many of East Anglia's finest eateries as well as a growing number of national customers, such as Tom Aikens, Cannon & Cannon of Borough Market and Jimmy's Farm Butchery. Besides unique products such as pig's cheek bacon, mutton bacon, chiang mai sausage and cotechino, Fruit Pig also produces the region's only fresh blood black pudding – a silver medal winner at France's international black pudding championships, and more recently a winner of the Great Taste Awards.'

Matt Cochin, The Fruit Pig Company

makes 8

SCOTCH EGGS

8 quail's eggs
75g pork sausagemeat
100g black pudding
50g pancetta
1 tsp fresh sage, finely chopped
Salt and freshly ground pepper
60g plain flour
1 medium hen's egg, beaten
50g fresh breadcrumbs
    blitzed with 25g jumbo oats
Vegetable or rapeseed oil,
    for deep-frying

SALAD CREAM

2 hard-boiled large eggs, yolks only
2 tbsp English mustard powder
Half a lemon, juice
1 tbsp caster sugar
3 tbsp white wine vinegar
150ml double cream
150ml rapeseed or sunflower oil

For the salad cream, blitz the cooked egg yolks with the other ingredients until thick and creamy, then slowly drizzle in the oil while the machine is still running until the dressing thickens. Taste and season, and add a little extra sugar if the salad cream is too sharp. Keep in the fridge.

Cook the quail's eggs for 2 minutes in a pan of boiling water, then drain and refresh in a bowl of iced water.

Blend the sausagemeat, black pudding, pancetta, sage and seasoning in a food processor on pulse until well combined.

Peel the eggs and shape the black pudding mixture around them to form small balls. Dredge each Scotch egg in the flour, roll in the beaten egg, then coat in the bread-and-oat crumb mix.

Heat the oil in a deep heavy-bottomed pan until a breadcrumb sizzles and turns brown when dropped into it. Carefully place each Scotch egg into the hot oil using a slotted spoon. Deep-fry for 3–4 minutes until golden-brown and crisp and the sausagemeat is cooked. Remove from the oil with a slotted spoon and drain on kitchen paper.

Homemade salad cream is well worth it – a great combination with this dish and others too.

Rare-breed hock terrine

'We have owned and run the Market Bistro on the Saturday Market Place in King's Lynn for the past four years. We have a simple philosophy of serving good food at affordable prices. We cook the best of Norfolk's ingredients, making everything from scratch here in our little kitchen. We were recently given a maximum three-star sustainability rating by the Sustainable Restaurant Association (SRA), placing us among the best performers in the UK. The award recognises our commitment to serve customers the most sustainably sourced food while also playing an active part in the community.'

Lucy and Richard Golding, Market Bistro, King's Lynn

serves 8–10

HOCKS

3 rare-breed ham hocks

6 carrots, chopped into chunks

2 leeks, chopped into chunks

6 onions, chopped into chunks

4 garlic cloves

2 bay leaves

6 cloves

2 blades mace

2 star anise

TO ASSEMBLE

1 sheet gelatine

130g gherkins

100g shallots

4g Colman's mustard powder

2g spice mix

SPICE MIX

6g onion powder

3g white peppercorns

6g paprika

2g allspice

3g black peppercorns

1.5g garlic powder

First make the spice mix. Toast all the spices briefly in a dry frying pan. Grind them in a spice grinder, then keep in an airtight container.

Put the ham hocks and all the flavouring ingredients into a 12-litre pressure cooker, cover with water, bring the cooker to full pressure and hold for $1^1/_2$ hours.

Release the pressure and remove the hocks. Strain the cooking liquor and reserve 1 litre for this recipe (freeze the rest for another use).

Soften the gelatine in cold water, then add to the cooking liquor in a saucepan over a medium heat and reduce to 500ml. Meanwhile, pick the meat from the hock bones, being careful not to include any tough sinew; try to retain some of the fat from beneath the skin, which gives a sweetness to the terrine. Carefully flake the meat, taking care not to overwork it.

Finely dice the gherkins and shallots, rinse under cold water and drain on kitchen paper.

Mix the shredded hock, gherkins, shallots, mustard powder and spice mix together in a large bowl. Add the reduced stock slowly until the meat is moist but not wet.

Double line a 1.5-litre terrine mould with cling film and pack the hock meat into the mould. Wrap the top with cling film and compress with a heavy weight. Refrigerate for a day. Remove the terrine from the cling film and slice. Serve with pickles and toast.

If you don't own a pressure cooker, put the hocks in a pan with the stock ingredients, cover with cold water and bring to the boil over a high heat. Reduce and simmer for 3 hours.

Seething pheasant rillettes

'Brasted's is known for its fine quality food and service within Norfolk and has a thirty-year reputation for creating the perfect party. We pride ourselves on using regional suppliers from in and around Norfolk. It is important to us to use local businesses as they help us to provide the very best seasonal provender. Often sought after to provide canapé parties at private venues in Norfolk and beyond, Brasted's has created an enviable and tantalising array of eats. The canapés here are firm favourites.'

Brasted's

makes 20–30

1 pack filo pastry

50g butter, melted

2 carrots

1 leek

2 sticks celery

1 garlic clove

2 onions

1 whole Norfolk pheasant

COMPOTE

500g mixed autumn berries

100g caster sugar

Vanilla pod, split

BREAD SAUCE

300ml fresh milk

5 peppercorns

3 thyme sprigs

2 bay leaves

2 star anise

4 cloves

6 slices white bread, crusts removed

Salt and freshly ground pepper

The rillettes can also be made as individual portions – four 8cm ramekins –and served with the berry compote and fresh crusty bread.

Preheat the oven to 180°C/fan 160°C/gas 4.

Brush one sheet of filo pastry at a time with melted butter. With a sharp knife cut into 5x5cm squares. Butter mini muffin tins and line each one with 3 buttered filo pastry squares placed at angles to one another to create a star shape. Bake until golden brown for about 10–12 minutes, then gently remove from the moulds and leave on a wire rack to cool.

Preheat the oven to 175°C/fan 155°C/gas 3½.

Finely dice the carrots, leek, celery, garlic and 1 onion. Put into a deep, lidded roasting dish, sit the pheasant on top, cover with water and put the lid on. Braise for 2½ hours. Remove from the oven and set aside to cool. Pick and shred the meat from the bones. Strain the liquid and reduce by half, skimming off excess fat from the top. Leave to cool. Once cool, add it back to the pheasant meat and press into a deep dish or terrine mould.

For the autumn berry compote, put the mixed berries into a pan with the caster sugar and vanilla pod. Reduce slowly until all the juices from the fruit have been released, then remove from the heat and set aside to cool.

For the bread sauce, put the milk in a saucepan with the peppercorns, thyme, bay leaves, star anise and the other whole, peeled onion, which you have studded with the cloves. Place on the heat to infuse for 7–10 minutes, then remove the pan, cover with a lid and set aside for 10–20 minutes to infuse further.

Remove the onion, bay leaves and star anise. Blitz the slices of bread into breadcrumbs, add to the milk, return to the heat and simmer for 6 minutes. Season to taste.

To assemble, spoon the bread sauce into the filo basket and top with teaspoon quenelles of pheasant rillettes. Garnish with a little compote.

Spicy goosegog chutney

'We started our business in 2012, hand-producing a range of award-winning chutneys, from our 2-Gold Star Parsnip & Chilli Chutney, to Norfolk Crier Onion Marmalade, named in honour of my husband, who peels my onions and cries. There is also our seasonal chutney, Pickled Samphire, and many more. A big thank-you to all the growers from our fantastic county because without them and their amazing produce we wouldn't be able to make our very special chutneys.'

Candi Robertson of Candi's Chutney

makes approximately 4kg

2kg gooseberries, topped and tailed

1kg dark brown sugar

500g white onions, chopped

500ml white malt vinegar

200g fresh root ginger, chopped

3 tsp cayenne pepper

2 tsp cumin seeds, ground

2 tsp coriander seeds, ground

2 tsp sea salt

Put all the ingredients into a large pan and slowly bring to the boil until all the sugar has dissolved. Remember to stir well as the chutney can easily catch on the bottom of the pan.

Turn the heat right down and simmer the chutney for approximately 1½ hours or until the chutney has thickened. At this point it is important only to stir the chutney occasionally.

Once cooked, pour into hot, sterilised jars. Store the chutney in a cool, dark, dry place for 4 weeks to mature.

Use a stainless steel pan and wooden spoon – other materials may react with the vinegar and cause discolouration.

Plum & cardamom jelly

'I love food, good food, the natural stuff we find all around us in our beautiful county of Norfolk. I have also travelled a lot and bring other influences to bear on my recipes. When I was in Hong Kong I tried Strawberry & Rose Jam and it blew me away. It is part of what inspired me to set up Essence Foods. We make high-fruit, reduced-sugar conserves using herbs and flowers to enhance the fruit flavours. All our products contain natural ingredients. This plum and cardamom jelly is sensational, whether with scones or as a glaze for duck or venison.'

Sarah Savage, Essence Foods

makes approximately 1.8kg

1.8kg plums with a good bold flavour

3 tsp cardamom seeds

300ml water

Approximately 1kg preserving sugar or 450ml pectin stock with 1kg plain granulated sugar

Cut the plums in half and remove the stones. Keep the stones in with the mixture.

Place the halved plums, stones, cardamom seeds and water in a pan and bring to the boil. Cover and gently simmer for 30 minutes to 1 hour until the plums are very soft. Cool slightly.

Carefully pour the contents of the pan into a sterilised/scalded jelly bag suspended over a large bowl. Leave to drain overnight.

Measure the resulting juice into a clean pan, adding 250g sugar for every 600ml of liquid.

Gently heat the mixture, stirring until the sugar has completely dissolved. Increase the heat and boil, without stirring, for 10–15 minutes. Setting point should be 105°C. You can also check for a 'good set' by placing a small amount of juice on to a saucer and putting it in a cold place – if the juice wrinkles when nudged with your finger, it is ready to pot.

Skim off any scum. Pour into warm sterilised jars, cover and seal. Store in a cool dark place and use within 1 year. Once opened, refrigerate and eat within 2 months.

You can also use the jelly to deglaze a roasting pan: a couple of spoonfuls and a glug of red wine will make a fantastic sauce for venison.

drinks

TEA & ICED TEA

'Wilkinson's have been blending tea and roasting coffee in the heart of Norwich since 1972. Still a small family business, we have built up a fine reputation for the quality of our delicious blends. There are many teas to choose from, but perhaps the most traditional afternoon tea has to be Earl Grey – and Wilkinson's at that. We blend our Earl Grey to an original recipe of Mr Wilkinson, created in the early 1970s. Its proportions are secret but it contains finest black China and Darjeeling, a suggestion of jasmine blossoms and is scented with pure oil of bergamot.'

Wilkinson's Tea and Coffee Merchants

The perfect cup of tea

Draw fresh water from the mains and set to boil. Before it boils, rinse the teapot with hot water to cleanse and warm it and add – the traditional guidance – 1 teaspoon of tea per person and 'one for the pot'. Loose-leaf tea gives a better flavour by far; the leaves can swim around the pot.

Immediately the water boils, pour on to the tea, stir and let it brew for 3–4 minutes. Pour through a strainer into your cup. Milk in first? Well, the debate will never end . . . Or try a slice of lemon, lime or even ginger in your teacup instead. Serve in Grandma's best china, raise your little finger and savour.

Iced tea

An alternative for a rare hot summer's day is iced tea, refreshingly different and thirst quenching. It's best to make your tea in advance, a few hours or even the night before, and let it go cold. A flavoured or scented tea gives best results. At Wilkinson's we have a large selection of the pure fruit teas based on hibiscus, which yields a rich, burgundy-coloured and fruity brew: strawberry & kiwi, apple & lemon, woodland berries, and many others.

So, choose your tea and be generous with the quantities, at least 3 tablespoons per pint of boiling water for a rich, concentrated infusion. Add sugar to the hot liquid if desired, leave to go cold and do not strain (yet). Shortly before required, pour the tea through a mesh strainer into a jug. Take another large glass jug and fill one-third to half full with ice cubes. Pour on the cold tea, add some sliced summer fruits, a sprig of mint (like a non-alcoholic Pimms), stir and serve. A naughty adult twist is to add a generous slug of vodka.

You can, of course, use a traditional tea: Earl Grey mixed with plum tea or an exotic green jasmine, for example. Or why not suggest a new blend for our shop? With over 150 teas at Wilkinson's, you have plenty to choose from.

COFFEE & COCKTAIL

'Grey Seal Coffee is a small batch coffee roastery based in Glandford, a hamlet in the Glaven Valley in North Norfolk. We ethically source and freshly roast green coffee beans to sell to the public and to the wholesale trade around Norfolk and throughout the UK. Our wonderful location, on a farmyard just off the coast in North Norfolk, is possibly the most rural setting for a coffee roastery and lab. We love to roast, brew, drink and talk about coffee. The Grey Seal Roastery is perfectly equipped to allow us to indulge our passions and share them with others.'

Grey Seal Coffee

Cold brew coffee

Cold-brewed coffee is refreshing, smooth and fruity and a perfect pick-me-up on a warm day. The following recipe can be made using any coffee. We recommend using a single origin, light/medium-roasted bean. Once brewed, this coffee can be kept in the fridge for up to 2 weeks.

Weigh 250g single-origin coffee beans and grind finely. Place in the bottom of a large jug or container. Gently pour 1 litre cold filtered water on to the coffee grounds, ensuring that all the coffee is evenly soaked. Carefully submerge any dry grounds that float to the surface. Leave for 8 hours to brew undisturbed.

Line a sieve with a muslin cloth or large filter paper, place over an empty vessel and slowly pour the brewed coffee through the filter. Pour into a large serving jug with plenty of ice, and enjoy.

Once you have made your cold-brew coffee, you can have a lot of fun making all sorts of coffee drinks.

Grey Seal cocktail

2 parts cold-brew coffee · 1 part crème de cassis · 1 part spiced rum · 3 dashes Angostura bitters

Amount per serving

This is our signature cocktail.

We use a single-origin Sumatran Mandheling bean to give an earthy yet fruity base.
Pour all the liquids into a cocktail shaker with plenty of ice and shake thoroughly.
Pour into a Martini or shallow cocktail glass and enjoy immediately.

For good coffee, use freshly roasted, good quality coffee. If at all possible, grind your own coffee (this keeps it even fresher). Never brew coffee with boiling water and make sure it is filtered first. Store your coffee in an airtight container in a cool dry place. Always be willing to try something new.

APPLE JUICES

Ashill Fruit Farm is a small, family-run fruit farm based in Ashill, Norfolk. The Reid family grow over forty varieties of apples, pears, plums and soft fruits. They produce a range of delicious cloudy apple with pear juices, pressed and bottled at the farm using their own fruit. They also have a range of own-label pickles, preserves and cider vinegar, for sale at the farm shop on site.

Norfolk Pure Apple Juice

Mulled apple juice with a kick

This delicious winter warmer is ideal to share with friends and family at dinner parties, Halloween, bonfire night and, of course, Christmas. One of the great advantages of this recipe is if you don't drink it all in one go it can be reheated and served again. The longer you leave it simmering, the stronger the flavours get.

serves 6

2 x 750ml bottles
  Sweet Cox Orange Pippin
  Norfolk Pure Apple Juice

4 cinnamon sticks

2 mulling spice bags

4 cloves

1 orange, zest

75ml cognac

Orange, sliced, to serve

Pour both bottles of juice into a large saucepan and add the cinnamon sticks, spice bags and cloves. Bring to boil, then turn down immediately. Add the zest and simmer for at least 30 minutes. Just before serving, add the cognac and pour through a sieve into heatproof glass mugs. Garnish with slices of orange.

Orchard mist

This refreshing non-alcoholic drink is a taste of the Norfolk countryside, bursting with pear and elderflower flavours. In springtime, when the pear trees are in bloom, garnish your glass with pear blossom. Outside springtime, a slice of lemon makes a perfect garnish.

Amount per serving

60ml Norfolk Pure Pear
  with Apple Juice

10ml lemon juice

30ml elderflower cordial

Half a lime

Half an orange

Fill a shaker with ice and add the apple juice, lemon juice and elderflower cordial, and shake until cold. Pour into a long or Martini glass over ice and top up with a squeeze of lime and orange.

Sandringham autumn cocktail

The first orchards at Sandringham were planted by King George VI and the farm has been producing apples ever since. Recently the orchards have been let to Andrew Jarvis, who has set up a new venture called Sandringham Apple Juice. Andrew manages about 12 hectares of orchard and produces apple juice from the factory on the estate. Eight varieties of apple juice are made: Discovery (sweet), Katy (medium sweet), Worcester Pearmain (medium sweet), Laxton's Fortune (sweet with a hint of pears), Cox (medium sweet), Egremont Russet (medium sweet with a slightly nutty taste), Howgate Wonder (medium dry) and Bramley (dry).

Sandringham Apple Juice

Amount per serving

25ml Sandringham Apple Spirit
(apple brandy)

75ml Sandringham
Discovery Apple Juice

75ml lemonade or soda,
according to taste

Slices of lime and fresh apple

Crushed ice

Put all the ingredients into a cocktail shaker, shake for 30 seconds, then pour. For parties, stir in a tall jug.

Add fresh ginger to give a warm kick to this lovely drink.

WINE
aka tea without the tea . . .

'Since taking on The Crown, William Mason Fine Wines have been committed to sourcing Norfolk produce. Initially we looked at the food aspect; this naturally led us on to the cellar. English sparkling wines have a reputation for quality because of the climate and terrain. In our Norfolk review we discovered the Winbirri Vineyard in Surlingham. This is a highly professional set-up and it was a revelation to try red, white and rosé wines that are extremely well made, using traditional methods.'

The Team at William Mason Fine Wines & The Crown at Great Ellingham

Wines

Set the challenge of pairing wines with afternoon tea, we thought long and hard about which wines from Winbirri would best complement this very English tradition of sandwiches, delicious cakes, scones, meringues, biscuits and tarts.

After extensive tastings and sandwich eating, we came to the conclusion that, for afternoon tea with a difference, the sparkling wine from Winbirri Vineyards, alongside a classic smoked salmon and cream cheese sandwich, is the answer.

We also found that rosé and cucumber sandwiches were not such a bad combination, while a heartier venison parfait goes down very nicely with Winbirri's light and fruity red. A glass of sweet sherry or Madeira also turned out to be rather good with a sumptuous raspberry cake or even a very traditional cream-filled scone.

Having thought it would be difficult to pair wines with afternoon tea, we have now decided that afternoon tea without the tea is, after all, a rather perfect thing.

contributors

ABEL ENERGY
Providing innovative and custom-designed renewable solutions to suit energy demands across Norfolk, Suffolk and East Anglia
Neaton Business Park North, Norwich Road, Watton, Norfolk IP25 6JB
01953 884486 info@abelenergy.co.uk
www.abelenergy.co.uk

ADEPT DESIGN
Design and digital agency for charities
15 White Hart Street, Aylsham, Norfolk NR11 6HG
01263 734198 hello@adeptdesign.co.uk
www.adeptdesign.co.uk

ALFRED G PEARCE
Suppliers of fresh produce and fine foods to restaurants and caterers
Garage Lane Industrial Estate, Setchey, King's Lynn, Norfolk PE33 0BE
01553 810456 info@alfredgpearce.co.uk
www.alfredgpearce.co.uk

ALICE SYZLING
Resident of Croxton for 100 years, superb home baker
Thetford, Norfolk

ARTHUR HOWELL
Family butchery business established in Binham in 1889
53 Staithe Street, Wells-next-the-Sea, Norfolk
01328 711300 office@arthurhowell.com
www.arthurhowell.com

BARSBY PRODUCE
Distinguished Norfolk wholesale supplier of fresh produce and fine foods
Old Meadow Road, Hardwick Ind Est, Kings Lynn, Norfolk PE30 4JZ
01553 772348 sales@barsbys.co.uk www.barsbys.co.uk

BETHANY REDHEAD
Young pastry chef sponsored by local charity
48 Yarmouth Road, Blofield, Norwich, Norfolk NR13 4LG

BISHOP OF NORWICH
Bishop's House, Norwich, Norfolk NR3 1SB

BLAKENEY HOTEL
A luxury north Norfolk hotel with quayside location
The Quay, Blakeney, Holt, Norfolk NR25 7NE
01263 740797 enquiries@blakeneyhotel.co.uk
www.blakeney-hotel.co.uk

BRASTED'S
Restaurant, hotel, catering and events company
Manor Farm Barns, Framingham Pigot, Norfolk NR14 7PZ
01508 491112 enquiries@brasteds.co.uk
www.brasteds.co.uk

BRAY'S COTTAGE PORK PIES
Award-winning pork pies made in a converted flint barn overlooking the sea
12 Bayfield Brecks, Holt, Norfolk NR25 7DZ
01263 712958 info@perfectpie.co.uk
www.perfectpie.co.uk

BREAD WORKSHOPS
Breadmaking workshops, teaching the craft of artisan bread
Holly Farm, Bressingham, Norfolk IP22 2BG
01379 688374 info@breadworkshops.co.uk
www.breadworkshops.co.uk

BRITONS ARMS
Long-established venue in the lovely historic part of Norwich
9 Elm Hill, Norwich, Norfolk NR3 1HN
01603 623367 britonsarms@gmail.com
www.britonsarms.co.uk

BUNNING'S FISH
Family-run fish shop and market stalls in the heart of Norfolk
Meadow Cottage, Cranworth, Hingham, Norfolk IP25 7SH
01362 820702 info@bunningsfish.co.uk
www.bunningsfish.co.uk

BUNS OF FUN
Homemade cakes and buns for any occasion
Sheringham, Norfolk NR26 8RP
0793 2874576 bunsoffunlovepots@hotmail.co.uk
www.bunsoffun.vpweb.co.uk

BYFORDS
All-day café and B&B in Holt's oldest building
Shirehall Plain, Holt, Norfolk NR25 6BG
01263 711400 queries@byfords.org.uk
www.byfords.org.uk

CANDI'S CHUTNEY
Producer of unique, award-winning chutneys
3 Foundry Close, Foulsham, Norfolk NR20 5TJ
01362 683348 candis1@aol.com
www.candischutney.vpweb.com

CERES BOOK SHOP
Bookshop and tea room
20 London St, Swaffham, Norfolk PE37 7DG
01760 722504 ceresbooks@aol.co.uk
www.ceresbookshopswaffham.co.uk

CHILLIS GALORE
Quality chilli products made by hand at home
in Norfolk
182A Drayton High Road, Drayton, Norfolk NR8 6BA
07824 508348 Kathy@chillisgalore.co.uk
www.chillisgalore.co.uk

CITY COLLEGE NORWICH
Catering and hospitality training
to the highest standards
Ipswich Road, Norwich, Norfolk NR2 2LJ
steven.thorpe@ccn.ac.uk www.ccn.ac.uk

COCOES
Café and deli offering fresh, wholesome, nourishing
and delicious food
STRATTONS
Ash Close, Swaffham, Norfolk PE37 7NH
01760 725605/723845 enquiries@strattonshotel.com
www.strattonshotel.com

CONGHAM HALL
Hotel and spa in 30 acres of parkland
Grimston, Kings Lynn, Norfolk PE32 1AH
01485 600250 info@conghamhallhotel.co.uk
www.conghamhalllhotel.co.uk

CORNERWAYS NURSERY
Tomato growers
Cornerways, Wissington, Stoke Ferry, Norfolk PE33 9RS
01366 500999 info@cornerwaysnursery.com
www.cornerwaysnursery.com

CROWN HOTEL
A former coaching inn tucked away in the fishing
port of Wells-next-the-Sea
The Butlands, Wells-next-the-Sea, Norfolk NR23 1EX
01328 710209 info@flyingkiwiinns.co.uk
www.flyingkiwiinns.co.uk

DUCK INN
Gastropub with regional ingredients
The Duck Inn, Burnham Road, Stanhoe, Kings Lynn
Norfolk PE31 8QD
01485 518330 info@duckinn.co.uk www.duckinn.co.uk

EDWARDS AND BLAKE LTD
Boutique contract caterer
1 Beacon House, Turbine Way, Swaffham,
Norfolk PE37 7XD
01760 72020 dholbeche-smith@edwardsand
blake.co.uk
www.edwardsandblake.co.uk

ENGLISH WHISKY CO
First whisky distillery in England for over 100 years
Harling Road, Roudham, Norfolk NR16 2QW
01953 717939 info@englishwhisky.co.uk
www.englishwhisky.co.uk

ESSENCE FOODS
Award-winning producer of artisan conserves
Salle Moor Farm, Wood Dalling Road, Reepham,
Norfolk NR10 4SB
01362 668844 info@essencefoods.co.uk
www.essencefoods.co.uk

FRUITPIG COMPANY

Artisan butchers using traditional breeds
Business Units 33–41, Boleness Rd, Wisbech,
Cambs PE13 2RB
0845 5480046 enquiries@fruitpigcompany.com
www.fruitpigcompany.com

ANTONY GORMLEY
AND VICKEN PARSONS

Artists
Norfolk

GRESSINGHAM FOODS

Red Tractor-assured farms in East Anglia rearing
the remarkable Gressingham Duck®
Loomswood Farm, Debach, Woodbridge,
Suffolk IP13 6JW
01473 735456 feedback@gressinghamfoods.co.uk
www.gressinghamduck.co.uk

GREY SEAL COFFEE

Freshly roasted, single-origin coffee from the
North Norfolk coast
Manor Farm Barns, Glandford, Norfolk NR25 7JP
01263 740249 david@greysealcoffee.com
www.greysealcoffee.com

G'S FRESH

Grower and packer of fresh salads and vegetables
G's Head Office, Barway, Ely, Cambs PE33 9RD
01353 727200 info@gs-fresh.com www.gs-fresh.com

GURNEYS FISH SHOP

Array of locally sourced fish in renowned
Burnham Market
Market Place, Burnham Market, Kings Lynn,
Norfolk PE31 8HF
01328 738967 www.gurneysfishshop.co.uk

GUY PATERSON

CLA Game Chef of the Year 2014,
farmer, stalker, chef
Dilham, Norfolk

HEYDON VILLAGE TEA SHOP

Traditional tea shop in unspoilt village
The Street, Heydon, Norwich, Norfolk NR11 6AD
01263 587211 cindy.watson@sky.com
www.heydonvillageteashop.co.uk

HEYGATE FARMS

Home of Norfolk Peer potatoes
Snailspit Farm, Cley Road, Swaffham,
Norfolk PE37 8AE
01760 721814 swaffham@heygates.co.uk
www.heygatefarms.co.uk

IMPERIAL HOTEL

Four-star, family-owned hotel since 1933
with Café Cru, The Terrace and Sea Views
13–15 North Drive, Gt Yarmouth, Norfolk NR30 1EQ
01493 842000 reservations@imperialhotel.co.uk
www.imperialhotel.co.uk

INGHAM SWAN

Fine dining and luxury rooms in award-winning
14th-century coaching inn
Sea Palling Road, Ingham,
Norfolk NR12 9AB
01692 581099 info@theinghamswan.co.uk
www.theinghamswan.co.uk

INSTITUTE OF FOOD RESEARCH

Addressing the fundamental science of food and
health and focusing on the issues of food security,
diet and health, healthy ageing and food waste
Norwich Research Park, Colney Lane, Norwich,
Norfolk NR4 7UA
01603 255000 ifr.communications@ifr.ac.uk
www.ifr.ac.uk

JO C'S NORFOLK ALE

Micro brewery
The Old Store, Walsingham Road, West Barsham,
Fakenham, Norfolk NR21 9NP
01328 863854 brewery@jocsnorfolkale.co.uk
www.jocsnorfolkale.co.uk

KETTLE FOODS

Snack food manufacturer
Barnard Road, Bowthorpe, Norwich,
Norfolk NR5 9JP
0800 616996 info@kettlefoods.co.uk
www.kettlechips.co.uk

LAST BRASSERIE

Open for breakfast, lunch, tea and dinner in the
Golden Triangle of Norwich
103 Unthank Road, Norwich, Norfolk NR2 2PE
01603 625047 www.lastwinebar.co.uk

LAVENDER HOUSE

Bustling restaurant, cookery school
and training kitchen
Brundall, Norfolk NRI3 5AA
01603 712215, enquiries@thelavenderhouse.co.uk
www.thelavenderhouse.co.uk

LORD IVEAGH & ELVEDEN FARMS

A farming enterprise with a thriving inn and
courtyard restaurant, food shop and home
and garden shops
The Elveden Estate, Elveden, Thetford,
Norfolk IP24 3TJ
01842 890223 estate.office@elveden.com
www.elveden.com

M+A PARTNERS

Chartered accountants helping private clients
and businesses grow and prosper
The Close, Norwich, Norfolk NR1 4DJ
01603 227600 enquiries@mapartners.co.uk
www.mapartners.co.uk

MACARONS AND MORE

Patisserie based in Norwich's Royal Arcade
11 Royal Arcade, Norwich, Norfolk NR2 1NQ
01603 419506 contact@macaronsandmore.com
www.macaronsandmore.com

MAIDS HEAD HOTEL

4-star independent hotel of charm in the centre
of Norwich
20 Tombland, Norwich, Norfolk NR3 1LB
01603 209955 reservations@maidsheadhotel.co.uk
www.maidsheadhotel.co.uk

MARKET BISTRO

Informal family-run bistro, using seasonal
and sustainable produce
11 Saturday Market Place, Kings Lynn,
Norfolk PE30 5DQ
01553 771483 info@marketbistro.co.uk
www.marketbistro.co.uk

MARY KEMP

Cookery writer and demonstrator
Hill House Farm, East Harling, Norfolk NR16 2LL
01953 717670 cooking@marykemp.net
www.marykemp.net

MELINDA RAKER

Norfolk Patron of Marie Curie
Croxton Park, Thetford, Norfolk IP24 1LS
01842 766025 mer@croxtonpark.co.uk

MERMAID SANDELSON

Winner of the Brecks Bake-off
and rising cookery star
Narborough Hall, Main Rd, Narborough,
Norfolk PE32 1TE

MILL CAFÉ BAR & RESTAURANT

Family-owned, family-friendly, café bar
and restaurant
Norwich Road, Yaxham, Dereham, Norfolk NR19 1RP
01362 851182 info@themillnorfolk.co.uk
www.themillnorfolk.co.uk

MORSTON HALL

Michelin-starred hotel and restaurant
on the North Norfolk coast
Tracy and Galton Blackiston, Morston, Holt,
Norfolk NR25 7AA
01263 741041 reception@morstonhall.com
www.morstonhall.com

MRS TEMPLE

Artisan cheesemaker using milk from own herd
of Swiss Brown cows
Copys Green Farm, Copys Green, Wighton,
Wells-Next-the-Sea, Norfolk NR23 1NY
sjt@jftemple.co.uk

MULBERRY TREE

B&B hotel with quality restaurant and bar food
Station Rd, Attleborough, Norfolk NR17 2AS
01953 452124 relax@the-mulberry-tree.co.uk
www.the-mulberry-tree.co.uk

NEIL ALSTON

Farmer, chef, cookery demonstrator

NORFOLK CORDIAL

Luxury handmade cordials, made with fresh,
natural ingredients
19 The Street, Matlaske, Norwich, Norfolk NR11 7AQ
01263 570251 hello@norfolkcordial.com
www.norfolkcordial.com

NORFOLK COUNTY ASPARAGUS
Breckland growers of Jolly Good Asparagus!
WO and PO Jolly (Norfolk) Ltd, Roudham Farm,
Roudham, Norfolk NR16 2RJ
01953 717126 info@norfolk-asparagus.co.uk
www.norfolk-asparagus.co.uk

NORFOLK GLUTEN FREE CO. LTD
The first exclusively gluten-free shop in the UK
Hellesdon Barns, Hellesdon Hall Road, Norwich,
Norfolk NR6 5BB
0787 252 9379 Louisa@norfolkglutenfree.co.uk
www.norfolkglutenfree.co.uk

NORFOLK MEAD
Boutique hotel, venue, rosette-awarded restaurant
Church Loke, Coltishall, Norwich, Norfolk NR12 7DN
01603 737531 info@norfolkmead.co.uk
www.norfolkmead.co.uk

NORFOLK PURE APPLE JUICE
Family-run orchard producing own apple juices
Ashill Fruit Farm, Swaffham Road, Ashill, Thetford
Norfolk IP25 7DB
01760 440050 pureapplejuice@tiscali.co.uk
www.norfolkpureapplejuice.co.uk

NORFOLK QUAIL LTD
Producers of ethically farmed quail meat and eggs
Highfield Farm, Great Ryburgh, Fakenham,
Norfolk NR21 7AL
01328 829249 enquiries@norfolkquail.co.uk
www.norfolkquail.co.uk

NORFOLK SAFFRON
Growers of the world's most precious spice
21 Norton Street, Burnham Norton, Kings Lynn,
Norfolk PE31 8DR
sally@norfolksaffron.co.uk www.norfolksaffron.co.uk

OWSLEY-BROWN CATERING
Outside caterer for events, weddings and parties
Conkers, Common Road, W Bilney, Kings Lynn,
Norfolk PE32 1JX
01692 536225 debbiesmith@placeuk.com
www.placeuk.com www.owsley-brown.com

PICNIC FAYRE
Traditional shop in historic forge
The Old Forge, Cley next the Sea, Norfolk NR25 7AP
01263 740587 enquiries@picnic-fayre.co.uk
www.picnic-fayre.co.uk

PLACE UK LTD
Suppliers of quality fruits for food makers
and retailers
Church Farm, Church Road, Tunstead, Norwich,
Norfolk NR12 8RQ
01692 536225 debbiesmith@placeuk.com
www.placeuk.com

PYE BAKER OF NORWICH
Artisan baker
Unit 3&4, Aylsham Road Business Park,
183 Aylsham Road, Norwich, Norfolk NR3 2AD
01603 404030 www.pyebaker.co.uk

RG ABREY FARMS
Family-run extensive farm specialising in vegetables
Larkshall, East Wretham, Thetford, Norfolk IP24 1QY
01953 498863 rga@abrey-farms.co.uk
www.abrey-farms.co.uk

STELLA RIMINGTON
British author and former Director General of MI5
Norfolk

RIVERFORD ORGANICS
Producers and retailers of organic vegetable boxes,
delivered to your door in conjunction with:
BRECKLAND ORGANICS
Church Farm, Shropham, Norfolk NR17 1UL
graham@brecklandorganics.co.uk
www.riverford.co.uk

ROCKET HOUSE CAFÉ
Café with spectacular views of Cromer's East Beach
The Gangway, East Promenade, Cromer,
Norfolk NR27 9ET
01263 519126 rockethousecafe@hotmail.com
www.rockethousecafe.co.uk

ROGER HICKMAN
A fine-dining establishment serving modern
British food
79 Upper St Giles Street, Norwich, Norfolk NR2 1AB
01603 633522 info@rogerhickmansrestaurant.com
www.rogerhickmansrestaurant.com

SANDRINGHAM APPLE JUICE
Grower and manufacturer of apple juice and cider
The Juice Plant, Flitcham Hall Barns, Flitcham,
Kings Lynn, Norfolk PE31 6BY
07810 310757 info@sandringhamapplejuice.co.uk
www.sandringhamapplejuice.co.uk

SAVILLS
Chartered Surveyors
Hardwick House, Agricultural Hall Plain, Norwich,
Norfolk NR1 3FS
01603 229229 www.savills.com

SCOTT'S FIELD PORK
Home of Norfolk's finest rare-breed pork
Orchard House, Scotts Lane, Brookville, Thetford,
Norfolk IP26 4RD
07940 800275 scottsfieldpork@btinternet.com
www.scottsfieldpork@btinternet.com

SPONGE
Award-winning handmade cake company
Hempstead Road, Holt, Norfolk NR25 6DL
01263 711033 info@sponge.co.uk www.sponge.co.uk

STANGROOM BROS LTD
Family farm producing herbs, fruit and cereals
Hamrow Farm, Whissonsett, Dereham,
Norfolk NR20 5SX
01328 700291 office@stangroombrothers.co.uk
www.stangroombrothers.co.uk

STRATTONS HOTEL
A small, independent, family-run boutique hotel,
restaurant and café/deli showcasing great
local produce
Ash Close, Swaffham, Norfolk PE37 7NH
01760 723845 enquiries@strattonshotel.com
www.strattonshotel.com

THE CLAN TRUST
A farming charity supporting Norfolk
c/o Brown & Co, 25 Tuesday Market Place, Kings Lynn,
Norfolk PE30 1JJ
www.theclantrust.co.uk

THE PIGS
A 17th-century country pub with bags of character
Norwich Road, Edgefield, Holt, Norfolk NR24 2RL
01263 587634 info@thepigs.org.uk
www.thepigs.org.uk

TITCHWELL MANOR
Family-run boutique hotel
Titchwell, Nr Brancaster, Norfolk PE31 8BB
01485 210221 Margaret@titchwellmanor.com
www.titchwellmanor.com

WAYLAND FREE RANGE EGGS
Supplying fresh free-range eggs to hotels, pubs,
butchers, farm shops, catering establishments
and other retail outlets
Rookery Farm, Great Ellingham, Attleborough,
Norfolk NR17 1LB
01953 457393 info@waylandfreerange.com
www.waylandfreerange.com

WILDEBEEST
Long-established restaurant and bar
82/86 Norwich Road, Stoke Holy Cross, Norwich,
Norfolk NR14 8QJ
01508 492497 wildebeest@animalinns.co.uk
www.animalinns.co.uk

WILKINSON'S TEAS
Tea and coffee merchants of Norwich
5 Lobster Lane, Norwich, Norfolk NR2 1DQ
01603 625121 info@wilkinsonsofnorwich.com
www.wilkinsonsofnorwich.com

WILLIAM MASON FINE WINES
Local independent wine merchant
and The Crown at Great Ellingham
30 Church Street, Great Ellingham, Attleborough,
Norfolk NR17 1LE
01953 455 411 wines@williammasonfinewines.co.uk
www.williammasonfinewines.co.uk

STUART WOODHEAD
Marie Curie supporter with personal experience of
their care

YARE VALLEY OILS
The Mack family farm beside the Norfolk Broads
The Grange, Surlingham, Norwich, Norfolk NR14 7AL
01508 538206 info@yarevalleyoils.co.uk
www.yarevalleyoils.co.uk

YES PEAS
Pea promotion campaign
BGA House, Nottingham Road, Louth,
Lincs LN11 0WB
mailbox@peas.org www.peas.org

index

Recipe for the Marie Curie Norfolk's Own Cookbook

- Mix a patron of the charity with three Marie Curie fundraisers over a working lunch until idea for baking combined with fundraising arises

- Leave basic ingredients with county's two leading food promoters, broadcasters and demonstrators for two weeks, during which time they give rise to amazing idea for compiling glorious cookbook

- Formulate procedures allowing at least 18 months to source ingredients, prove and bake. Prepare to roll up sleeves and work hard at kneading, rolling, whisking and blending in order to create a quality product

- Begin method. Add 80 supportive contributors and combine with generous sponsors. Await recipes using the best of Norfolk produce, subscriptions and useful introductions. Beat the tardy gently with wooden spoon

- Source the best designer and a professional editor and add a good sprinkling of humour and knowledge from known publisher. Blend with proven printer of quality hardback books, squeezing gently to extract competitive costings

- Using accurate scales, maintain at least 16 lists combined with databases, spreadsheets and stringent budgets

- Test the recipes over several weeks, adjusting where necessary, finally introducing professional cookery photographer

- Fold all ingredients together with great care and dispatch to designer for baking. Remove and pass to editor for topping, returning to designer for sugar sprinkles finish

- Send completed proof to printer. Nervously await arrival of finished product

- Unwrap with great care. Distribute books to 5,000 hungry cooks. Sell each one for the same cost as one hour of Marie Curie nursing, which is provided free to those who need it. Realise that every sale will support the wonderful work of Marie Curie in Norfolk

MARY KEMP

Mary Kemp, cookery writer and demonstrator with a Norfolk farming background, is an advocate for locally produced, seasonal food made using the finest and freshest ingredients. Mary has been involved in the world of cookery for the last twenty-five years, expanding her knowledge and expertise at places such as Raymond Blanc's Le Manoir and Billingsgate Seafood School. She writes for the Norfolk magazine, is a regular guest on BBC Radio Norfolk and organises cookery theatres across East Anglia, showcasing the best local produce and chefs. Mary is a Nuffield Farming Scholar and has travelled extensively studying food and farming, being named Food Hero in the EDP 2013 Norfolk Food & Drink Awards. In recognition of her commitment, passion and support of the food and drink industry here in Norfolk, Mary has been appointed an Honorary Trustee of Norfolk Food & Drink Limited.

MELINDA RAKER

Melinda Raker has been involved with the family farming business in South Norfolk for more than forty years. She has worked with numerous charities over many years in formal roles and innovative fundraising. In 2008 she set up the YANA Project on behalf of the Clan Trust to raise mental health awareness among the farming communities of Norfolk and Suffolk. Melinda is Norfolk Patron of Marie Curie and believes passionately that those who are terminally ill should be able to remain in their own homes if they wish, supported by good palliative care. Her main aim as Patron in Norfolk is not just to raise funds for this very special charity but to raise the profile of the wonderful work of the Marie Curie nurses. Melinda is also a Trustee of the Norfolk Heart Trust and a Deputy Lieutenant of Norfolk.

left to right Mary Kemp, Vanessa Scott, Melinda Raker

VANESSA SCOTT

Vanessa Scott and her husband Les have been running the boutique hotel Strattons in Swaffham in the Norfolk Brecks since 1990, now joined by daughter Hannah and son-in-law Dominic. The site also includes a café/deli. Vanessa heads up the food operation, which has won considerable plaudits for both quality and her policy of sustainably sourcing ingredients. This approach has won the business national recognition. It became the first hotel in the UK to win the prestigious Queen's Award for Outstanding Environmental Performance and Green Globe's Best Small Global Hotel, and was the first restaurant in the UK to receive the RSPCA Ethical Food award.

Vanessa has also been named EDP Food & Drink Hero and Outstanding Achievement winner. In 2011 she spearheaded the first annual Brecks Food Festival, which won an Action for Market Towns award. She is a regular culinary contributor to Radio Norfolk's Garden Party and a patron of the Norfolk Food & Drink Festival.